Practical Writing Strategies

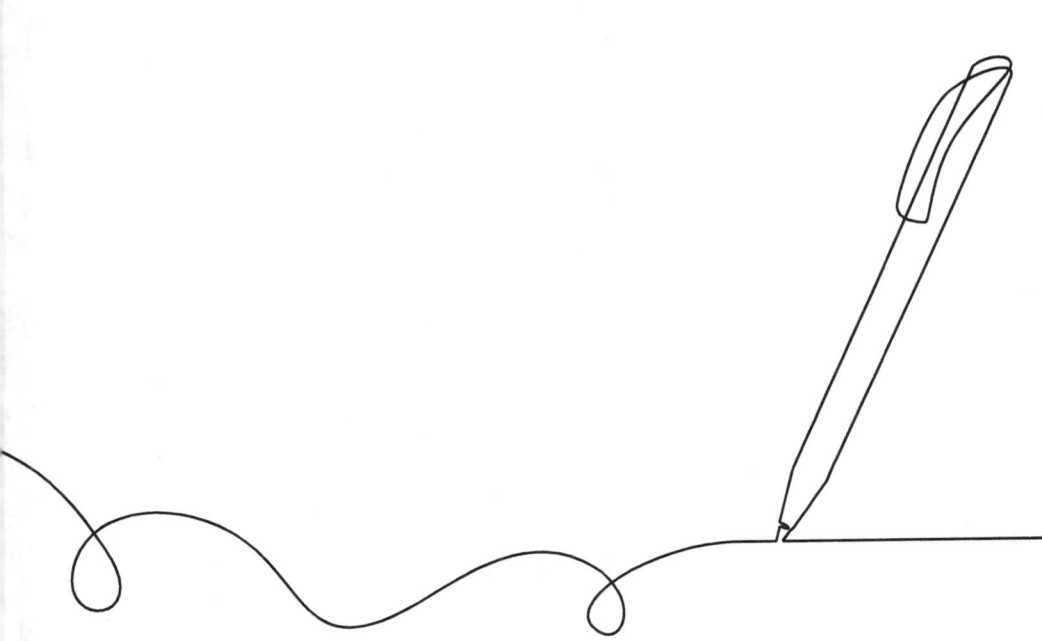

LEON FURZE and BENJAMIN WHITE

Practical Writing Strategies

Engaging Activities for Secondary Students

amba press

Copyright © Leon Furze and Benjamin White, 2023

All rights reserved. No part of this book may be reproduced or transmitted in any form or by any means, electronic or mechanical, including photocopying, recording or by any information storage and retrieval system, without prior permission in writing from the publisher.

Published by Amba Press
Melbourne, Australia
www.ambapress.com.au

Editor – Rica Dearman
Cover Designer – Tess McCabe

Printed by IngramSpark

ISBN: 9781922607508 (pbk)
ISBN: 9781922607515 (ebk)

A catalogue record for this book is available from the National Library of Australia.

For the kids – Leon
For Shaun – Ben

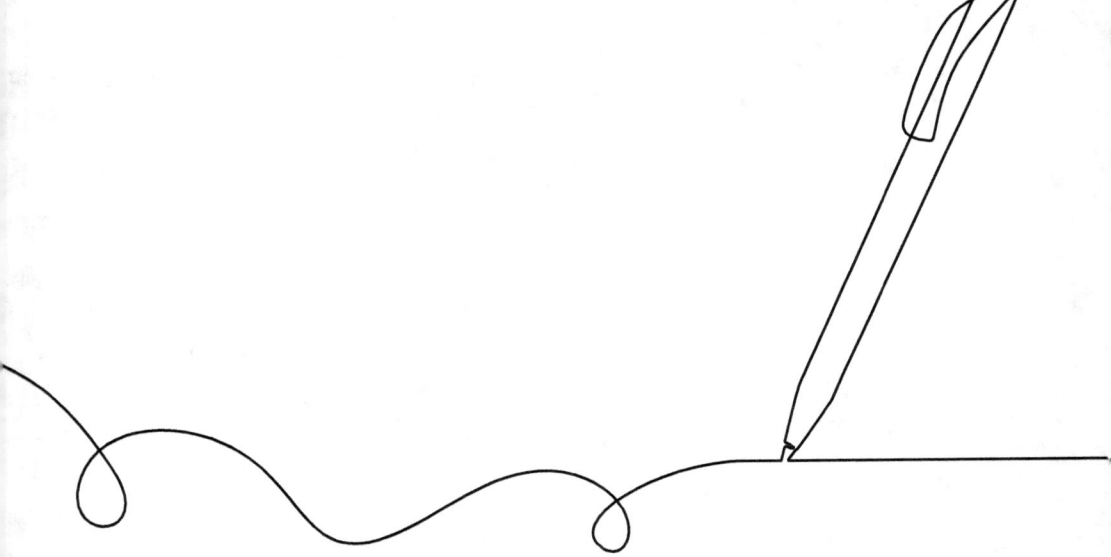

Contents

Acknowledgements		ix
Introduction		1
Part I		**11**
Chapter 1	Purpose	11
Chapter 2	Exploration	27
Chapter 3	Ideas	49
Chapter 4	Skills	65
Chapter 5	Collaboration	87
Chapter 6	Publication	103
Part II		**119**
Chapter 7	Constructing a unit of work	119
Chapter 8	Giving feedback	129
Chapter 9	Writing across the curriculum	139
Chapter 10	Being a writer	145
Chapter 11	Creating a culture of writing	151
Chapter 12	The future of writing	157
Conclusion		165
References		167

Acknowledgements

Leon

Practical Writing Strategies couldn't have happened without the support of my family – Emily and the kids. As I worked on its predecessor, *Practical Reading Strategies*, we went from one child to two. This time around, we went from two to three, which is sort of like going from six to a million. Family life is challenging enough without trying to cram another book in around the edges, and I couldn't have done it without support and kindness. The coffee machine that got me through the first book worked so hard that it broke, twice, and got replaced.

While *PWS* wasn't an outcome of a VATE Community of Practice like the first book, I'd still like to thank the association for providing the impetus and encouragement needed to keep writing. Contributing to VATE's *Idiom* magazine, presenting at conferences and taking part in VATE events has allowed me to test ideas and reach many more English teachers. The community which built up around *Practical Reading Strategies* also deserves a mention. Hundreds of English teachers supported the first book and, more importantly, made it their own, adapting and changing the activities to suit diverse cohorts and texts. I hope that happens again.

I'd like to once again thank Alicia Cohen at Amba Press and Rica Dearman who edited this book. Alicia took a punt with the first book and has been a supportive and vocal advocate throughout the whole process. Finally, thanks to my co-author and (former) colleague Ben, who never once complained about getting messaged at 6am with some random new idea.

Ben

Writing this has been a challenge. It always seems like a good idea to start a project like this at the time, and then the reality hits. Nevertheless, this has been a thoroughly rewarding experience.

Particular thanks must go to Shaun, who puts up with my being in the study, cheerfully ignoring all domestic duties because "I'm working!" Thanks to Alicia Cohen and Amba Press for their support and Rica Dearman for editing this work. Thanks to Leon for his guidance; I wish him well as he chases new ideas down the rabbit hole. Finally, a special thanks to all my students over the years who have been patient and tolerant of me trialling new activities in the classroom – their generosity of spirit knows no bounds.

I hope this book helps in some small way with the monumental task that all teachers play in and out of the classroom. I especially hope this book helps any graduate teachers who planned their lesson perfectly, but it didn't quite work out. May one of these activities save your lesson.

Introduction

What is writing?

When Leon wrote *Practical Reading Strategies*, he started with a seemingly simple question: what is reading? The question came from a Community of Practice run by the Victorian Association for the Teaching of English (VATE) and was used to explore what goes on 'behind the eyes' when students read. It quickly became apparent that the question was anything *but* simple.

When students read, any number of things might be going on: from a slow and methodical processing of individual words to full technicolour moving pictures in the imagination. *PRS* explored the 'what' and the 'why' of reading, and so it makes sense to begin this second book in the same place.

Reading draws on contextual cues, language knowledge and memories (Gee, 2004). Writing does all this, *plus* the added cognitive effort of focused attention, the selection of words and phrases, and the motor skills of actually putting pen to paper (or fingers to keyboard)

(Hermansson & Lindgren, 2019). Writing is a highly demanding act, and not something to be taken lightly.

And yet in schools we often try to shortcut the complex processes involved in writing in a race to get to the product – the written outcome itself. Our education system – driven along by standardised assessments and high stakes testing – seems to demand that we hurry along and get to 'the point'. Rather than carefully stepping through the required stages of writing – including reading and planning, generating ideas, drafting, refining and editing – students are often placed in the unfortunate position of having to write only by imitation. Formulaic essay structures, which should only be used as scaffolds, become the ultimate ends, and writing is reduced from a process to a product.

This is by no means the fault of teachers. In 'content-heavy' subjects, such as the Sciences and Humanities, examination pressures dictate that writing should be taught as a means to an end. Even in the English classroom the pressures of senior secondary assessment dominate the writing landscape, with essay structures reverberating down from Year 12 through to the junior levels.

But it doesn't have to happen this way. Writing is a complex process, and it should be treated with the time, care and attention it deserves. "Learning the craft of writing… enables writers to find their own 'voice'", and it is a slow and considered process (Carey et al, 2022, p36). *Practical Writing Strategies*, like the reading book that preceded it, encourages teachers to slow down, cut out content to focus on skills and lead students gently through the complex process of writing.

Shifting the focus

Our Writing Cycle was developed over years of trial and error. While we were focused on integrating the Reading Strategies into our curriculum, we deliberately shelved writing, making the controversial decision to greatly reduce the amount of time spent explicitly teaching writing. We predicted a temporary drop in our NAPLAN writing results, but this didn't play out. Our 2021 results – even after COVID-19 and remote learning – were marginally higher. We saw a dip in 2022 after the return to 'COVID-normal' saw us facing inconsistent staff and student absences. As a result, we'll never really know the full impact of shifting our focus away from writing based on Year 7 and 9 NAPLAN results.

Then, something surprised us. During the COVID years, we started to get the best Victorian Certificate of Education results we had seen. In Victoria, Year 12 students must complete at least one of the English studies. For us, roughly 80% of our students complete VCE English. In 2020 and 2021, we saw our best results in more than a decade, as measured by students in the high 30s and 40-plus scores, and also by students in the lower ranges drawing closer to the state average.

So, while the shift in focus away from writing and towards reading had no clear impact on NAPLAN, it seemed to have had a significant impact on our senior results. Comparing the kinds of essays students were writing in 2017 to those they write now, it's easy to see why. Focusing on close reading, discussing texts and prioritising student voice has resulted in writing that is much more vibrant and personal. *Practical Reading Strategies* explains how we got there.

With the Reading Strategies safely tucked under our belts, we started to shift our attention back to writing. Towards the end of 2020, we began to develop and refine a process of writing that was backed up by the Reading Strategies. As a result, we developed our Writing Cycle.

Process, product or genre?

When you start exploring the research around teaching writing, you'll inevitably come across debates about the various merits and faults of process writing, product writing and genre writing. It is worth exploring each of these methods.

Process writing

Process writing, as the name suggests, teaches writing as a process from ideas, through drafting, to editing and submission. Instruction is broken into clear stages, and typically eschews models or conventions in favour of continuous feedback and revision.

Product writing and genre writing

Product writing was the preeminent model of writing instruction in the UK, US and Australia until the 1960s and 1970s, after which it was largely supplanted by process writing. It begins with a model text, teaches the language and formal conventions, scaffolds practice of the skills, and directs students to create an original text using the conventions and techniques derived from the model. Genre writing builds on the product model, with more of a focus on the generic conventions. In genre writing, the language techniques highlighted by the product writing approach are grounded in the conventions of the genre.

We believe there is a false dichotomy between process and product – students need to be taught via both approaches. A focus on product writing can lead to decontextualised instruction, for example, of grammar or language techniques. On the other hand, research has pointed to evidence that process writing may disadvantage struggling writers (AERO, 2022, p14).

The Writing Cycle incorporates elements of both methods of instruction. Like process writing, it follows a clear structure to support students throughout the creation of their texts. Like product and genre writing, we use models (mentor texts) and explicit instruction of skills, which are contextualised by the texts they study in class.

Overview of the Writing Cycle

In the creation of the Writing Cycle we are indebted to several other authors and educators who have produced amazing work on writing as a process (for example, see Moon, 2011; Derewianka, 2015).

We developed the Cycle alongside the Reading Strategies, always coming from a position of reading first, writing later. Both authors of this text write regularly – Ben has written many texts for English teachers, and Leon writes both nonfiction and fiction. We know that writers read voraciously and that what we read colours our writing. But we also know that this is not the case for many of our students.

The Writing Cycle needed to address the fact that many students are starting from a disadvantaged position when it comes to putting their ideas down on paper or screen.

That's why the actual writing doesn't begin until somewhere between the third and fourth stages of the cycle, when students begin to draft. Prior to that, students engage in a lot of discussion, brainstorming, ideas generation and reading of other authors' texts.

Another important aspect was our understanding that the writing is never really 'finished'. We've both had experiences where the editor's deadline is the only thing stopping the writing from being in a state of eternal revision – folders cluttered with files called things like Chapter1_Final_Draft_v1..2.4.7a... As writers, we iterate through the stages, starting by identifying the purpose and audience, then coming up with some ideas, drafting, collaborating with peers and editors, and then reviewing the text to make sure it really *does* fit the purpose before moving through the cycle again. Eventually, the text reaches a point where it is fit for submission (or the deadline passes and the editors become agitated).

The Writing Cycle maps out these stages of the process, avoiding the temptation typical to education to skip straight from purpose (you need to write an essay) to publication (please submit the essay).

The Writing Cycle

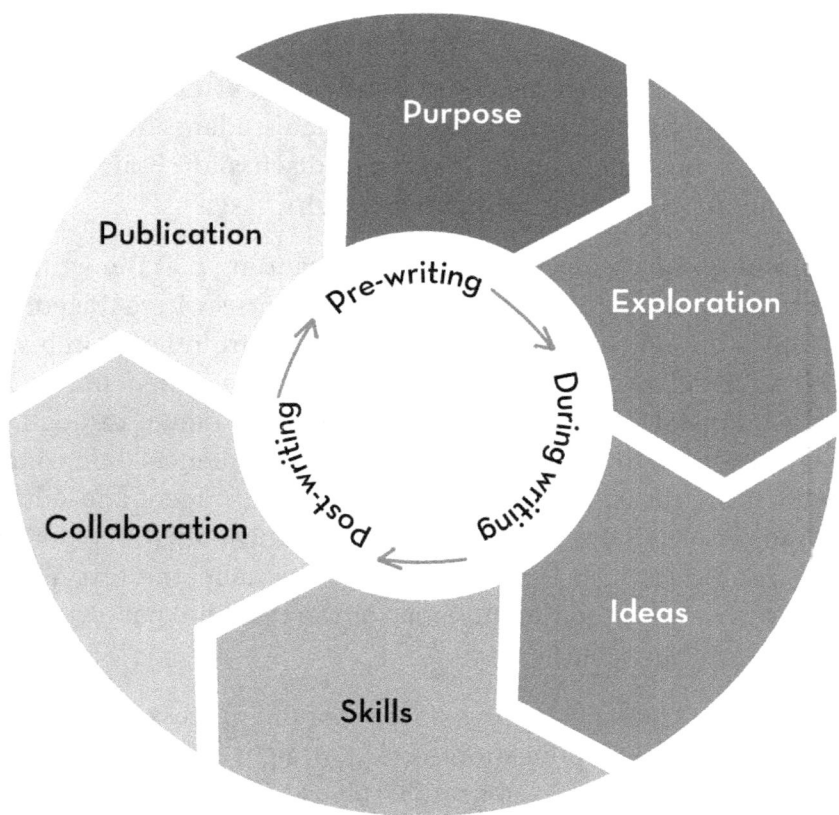

Purpose

This includes the reason for writing, the audience, the context and the motivation. Students, like any other writers, need more than just, 'because it is the required assessment outcome'. A clear purpose sets the tone for the rest of the writing.

Exploration

In the exploration stage, students play with texts, exploring multiple models of quality writing in order to get a feel for how other authors have approached similar purposes and audiences. This may include discussions on form, themes, genre or techniques.

Ideas

Writers generate ideas – brainstorming, discussions and collaboration encourages students to experiment and test ideas. In this stage, students might begin working on drafts.

Skills

All students write differently and have different needs. In this stage, students identify specific skills to focus on, which will support their writing. This might include work on vocabulary, technique, structure and so on.

Collaboration

Writing is rarely done in a bubble. Professional authors often rely on beta readers, editors, and friends and family for much-needed advice and support. Students work together in writing groups and with teachers to refine their ideas.

Publication

Publication might be the end of a single cycle, or a trigger to go back to *purpose* and review. Students may decide to explore further texts at this point or refine their ideas and skills. When the text is ready for submission, it will be published in the appropriate form.

How to use this book

Each stage of the Writing Cycle is demonstrated with four activities. These are examples of the kinds of activities writers might undertake in each stage of the cycle but are by no means the *only* activities that fit. We would encourage you to get familiar with these as the basics before starting to integrate your own ideas into the cycle. Part II of this book explores how to take the Writing Cycle and apply it to different areas of teaching, from a single unit of work to a whole curriculum.

Each chapter in Part I follows the same format of four activities, split into:

- Teacher instructions
- Student instructions
- Example
- Reflect
- Extend

Teacher instructions

In the teacher instructions you will find an overview of the resources (physical or digital) required to complete the activity, plus a step-by-step process including anything required before the lesson to set up. The teacher instructions are designed to be as comprehensive as possible, and sometimes include scripts for discussing the activity with students.

Student instructions

The student instructions are a condensed version of the instructions for teachers. They are deliberately concise so that they can be easily copied and shared with students. These instructions do not need to be handed out to students for every activity; sometimes the teacher's verbal instructions will suffice, and sometimes the framework or graphic organiser provided for the activity is self-explanatory.

Example

In the example section you will find a completed version of the task. Many of these are reproduced with permission from actual students. Some are an amalgam of various student responses that we have pulled together as an example. In all cases, the activities have been completed by real students and trialled and tweaked on more than one occasion. In some instances (such as those in the chapter on *Publication*), a complete example would be too large to include here and so extracts are used to demonstrate the key aspects of the activity.

Reflect

The reflection section of each activity is an important opportunity to think about the impact of the activity with *your* students. In some cases, it would be good to review the reflection prompts *before* completing the activity. For example, there are moments when you might wish to discuss the activity with your team and make some changes for your particular cohort of students beforehand. In other instances, the reflect questions encourage you to review how the activity went, and what could be done differently next time.

Extend

Each activity concludes with suggestions for how to extend. These could be opportunities for highly able students to push themselves further, or suggestions for follow-up activities. In some cases, the extend section may lead towards a summative task such as an essay or creative piece.

Part I

Chapter 1: Purpose

It is important that students understand the *purpose* of any project before they begin. As they grow in confidence, students might find that they are able to write first and wait for a purpose to 'emerge' from their writing – we often find this happens with prolific blog and article writers, for example. But in the early stages of their writing careers, it is helpful to have a clearly defined reason to write.

As we discussed in the introduction, there has been much debate as to the benefits of 'product writing' versus 'process writing'. This initial step – identifying the audience, purpose and context – is very much a process-driven stage. This does not mean that students cannot experiment and play around with form and genre – quite the opposite. Genre norms should be 'culturally situated' and 'dynamic' (Chapman, 1999). This means you should discuss the expected purpose, audience and context while being mindful of the experience and knowledge students themselves bring to the classroom. "Experimentation, with writing for real purposes and audiences, is thought to produce better writers" (McKnight, 2021) and the activities in the first two stages of the cycle help students understand the conventions of genres, and how and when to break them.

It is important to note that even these initial planning stages of the writing process benefit from clear instruction, scaffolding and support. Providing students with examples and guided instruction on *how* to identify and lock into the purpose of their writing is vital; you can't just tell students to 'plan' a piece of writing and leave it at that.

Steven Graham, in his essay on writing communities, discusses the importance of "how writing is conceptualised within a community in terms of purpose, including writing goals, norms and stance" (Graham, 2018). Students may think of the same text in many different ways based on their understanding of purpose and audience. If it is not made clear to them from the outset, this could lead to unintended results. Graham provides the example of a writing task about the connection between hip-hop and rhythm and blues music, and points out that students' work will vary dependent on their own musical knowledge and tastes, their personality, their physical and mental state at the time of writing, and many other factors. Because of this, it is doubly important to ensure the class has a clear and agreed upon starting point.

In this book, we divide the overall *purpose* of a text into three categories: purpose, audience and context.

Purpose

This is the reason for the text's existence. It may be something as simple as the function of the writing. Applebee (1984) suggested 'informational', 'personal' and 'imaginative' as suitable categories of writing. We tend to think in terms of texts that inform, explain, persuade and entertain. On the other hand, the purpose may be in response to an issue or event. The purpose might also be informed by the audience and context, just as much as it may inform those elements. The three components are closely connected, and students need to be aware of each before they begin writing if they are to produce something specific and considered.

Audience

The audience of the piece will inform many things, from the register or level of formality through to the genre and form. Often, particularly with persuasive writing, students hold only a vague idea of the audience in their minds, such as 'Australian teenagers'. The audience should be made as specific as possible if students are aiming for a piece that appeals emotionally or logically to the readers, whatever the purpose. In a 2022 review of the NAPLAN writing test, AERO report that "over one-third (38%) of Year 9 students achieved a score of 3 or less out of a possible 6 for the criterion addressing audience" (AERO, 2022, pxi). Irrespective of your opinions on NAPLAN (and we certainly all have those), it is true in our experience that students struggle to align their writing with a specific audience. This means it is important to teach them how to articulate their audience as clearly as possible.

Context

The who, what, when and where of the text will inform aspects such as the form and genre. For example, the same headline might generate a totally different response in two different newspapers. A blog post title might be used to inspire a creative piece for publication in a literary magazine, which might in turn provoke an analytical response. Students might also position their texts at different points in time, for example, writing within a historic period.

All these aspects combine to shape the initial ideas of the text. In the classroom, you will vary the amount of time spent covering each element dependent on the outcome you're seeking. For example, if students are going to write a persuasive piece, then audience, purpose and context are very important. On the other hand, if the task is to write a creative piece as a warm-up or to inspire future writing, you may not need to address anything beyond that statement of purpose.

ACTIVITY 1:
The Roadmap

When starting the Writing Cycle, students often struggle to find a real purpose, and thus struggle to find their motivation. Students need clarity when starting a new writing project. By offering students the chance to craft their own roadmap for their writing project, they're taking ownership of it.

Often, students will see submitting the task by the due date as a goal in and of itself. And while they're not wrong, it's important we emphasise that writing is a process, and processes by their very nature are broken down into discrete steps to follow. Having students assign themselves these goals and steps will help them with finding their motivation and keeping their motivation.

This strategy invites students to figure out a roadmap for their writing project. The emphasis is on short, achievable goals. Seeking feedback should also be encouraged; a true motivating force for students is the feedback of their peers.

Teacher instructions

1. Start by asking your students to think of the writing project they're currently working on (the essay, the oral presentation, creative or personal responses).
2. Next, have them consider specific, achievable goals for their writing project. Encourage them to move beyond 'get a high mark' and move towards things like 'write 200 words by the end of this lesson' or 'a first draft by the end of the week'. Have them create an achievable to-do list of tickable goals.
3. Once they have identified their goals, have them write them down. Encourage them to keep this list with them as they are writing. They can refer to it as they proceed with their project, and also get the thrill of ticking things off their list. Because, let's face it, there's no greater thrill than ticking things off the to-do list.
4. Finally, harness the power of supportive peers. Have students share their writing goals with the class. Students can discuss these goals with one another and build out their lists as a result of the discussions.

Student instructions

1. Think of your writing project. Consider all aspects: due dates, word length, criteria, the text you're writing on (if applicable).
2. Write down a list of achievable steps and goals for your writing project (for example, to have 200 words written by the end of this week). Think beyond 'getting a good score' and move towards things that you can tick off, a checklist of sorts.
3. Write your goals on a separate sheet of paper, something you can keep handy and close by; perhaps in your planner.
4. Share your goals with your peers.
5. As you move through your writing project, tick your goals off as you achieve them.

Example

> PERSONAL RESPONSE ASSESSMENT
> ☆WRITING GOALS☆
> ☐ Have outline written by Friday; conference with teacher.
> ☐ 200 words written by end of Monday's lesson
> ☐ Show BFF.
> ☐ Write another 200 words by Tues lesson
> ☐ Read over 400 words, edit.
> ☐ Write final 300 words. Edit.
> ☐ Ask teacher about Writer's Statement
> ☐ Complete Writer's Statement (150 w)
> ☐ Final read over + edit - Submit Friday of Week 6.

Reflect

- Have students reflect on how setting specific, achievable goals helped them to complete their task.
- This reflection, in the case of the Personal Response example above, could form a part of the task.

Extend

- This activity could be extended for students by having them create a range of checklists for other projects, perhaps in other subjects.
- Students could also create a range of generic checkpoints for future projects.

ACTIVITY 2:
Think Tank

One of the clearest purposes for students to understand is the persuasive text. Students are aware, going into this kind of writing project, that they must persuade someone of something. They need to 'sell' their idea. While the purpose of this kind of writing is clear and easily understood by our students, they often struggle with what exactly they're going to write on and speak about.

Often when approaching this kind of task, I ask my students to consider what they're passionate about, what fires them up. What do they want to see change in the world? In the classic teenage fashion, they often reply with "nothing fires me up". Endearing, but annoying.

This strategy invites students to consider a topic from multiple, personal perspectives – in much the same way a think tank might ruminate on the issue of the day. The goal being for students to settle on what their point of view on an issue is and how they arrived at that perspective. From there, students will be able to begin crafting their project.

Using a mentor text

Often at this point of the persuasive writing process, students are more in need of ideas or starting points for their writing, rather than models to follow. Consider sending students to various resources to get them thinking about what's happening in the world:

- *ABC News*
- *The Project*
- *The Guardian*
- *The Herald Sun*
- Local newspapers and social media sites, for local issues
- Interview the school's Student Leadership Team, or the principal

Teacher instructions

1. Provide students with a copy of the graphic organiser opposite or have them draw their own.
   a. Modelling this process on the board for class input will help students to grasp each step with greater clarity.
2. Students are to work through each circle and respond to each prompt.
   a. Move around the room, checking in with students and challenging some of their ideas.
3. Peer review and discussion should be encouraged at each step.

Student instructions

1. Think about your topic or issue and the aspect of it you're most connected to. There must be a reason you chose it, even if it seemed like 'the easiest option'.
   a. What do you really identify with?
   b. What can you confidently say, right now, about this topic or issue?
2. Print out or copy the graphic organiser to begin organising your thoughts.

Graphic organiser

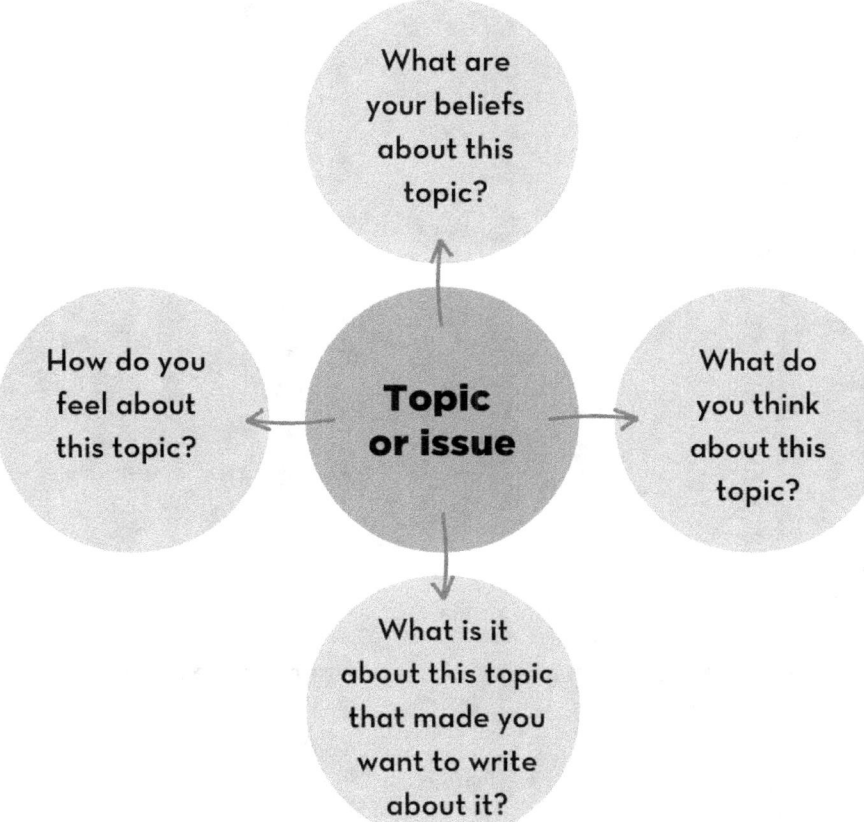

3. Now that you've unpacked what you really believe, think and feel about this topic or issue, you can focus your energy on writing *just* about that.

Example

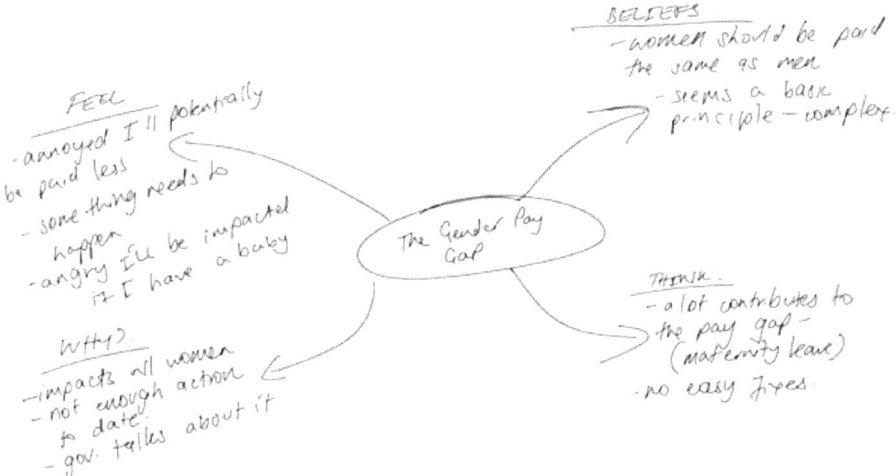

Reflect

✏️ Students should be encouraged to consider as many aspects as possible of their issue.

Extend

✏️ The possibilities for this activity are seemingly endless. As each bubble is refined down, more layers can be added. This will essentially be the makings of a persuasion map.

ACTIVITY 3:
Write for the Right Crowd

Now that students have *something* they're going to write about, it's important to figure out *someone* to write to. Often, students will settle on an issue and speak to as broad an audience as possible – a favourite being 'the government'. While this may suit some topics, it's a little broad. Consider: does the entirety of the government care about recycling bins? Probably not. It's likely only one department would care.

This strategy invites students to move beyond generalising their audience and towards specifically targeting *who* they will speak or write to. The goal being that once they have successfully reduced their audience to those who can enact change, they can then formulate their arguments. The choices they'll make in their writing will become clearer. With a clear purpose and a clear audience in mind, students will be more motivated to continue with the writing project.

While this strategy has been conceptualised around a persuasive writing piece, there's scope here to use it for any mode of writing. If the project is concentrated around fiction, for example, this strategy could be employed to settle on the appropriate audience (young adult, kids, senior citizens) and thus their language choices can be tailored appropriately.

Teacher instructions

1. Model each step of the process on the board.
    a. There's a theme developing with these strategies: modelling.
2. At each point, ask clarifying questions of the students; our favourite is: 'what makes you say that?'
3. Once students have refined their audience, they can then start looking at ways that they can engage with them.

Student instructions

What is your issue or topic?

↓

**Who are the stakeholders?
Who cares about this issue?**

| Who has the answer to your question? | Who can effect change? | Who has the answer to the problem you're trying to solve? |

↓

Congratulations, you've found your audience

| What motivates them? | What excites them? | What scares them? |

Example

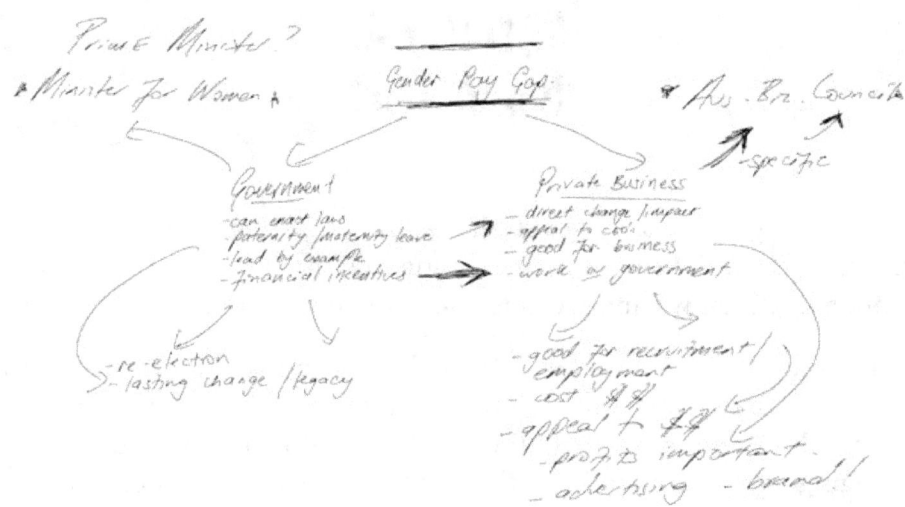

Reflect

In the example above, where the issue is the Gender Pay Gap, the student works through these steps with the teacher. Being an issue that impacts both government and business, the student worked through which audience they could target most effectively. In this case, the student settled on the Australian Business Council, as they were to think of more potential avenues – and arguments – for this audience.

Extend

This activity can be extended by having the student consider multiple audiences for their writing project. Instead of researching one, they might go through the process for different demographics and find that they're not only unpacking different demographics, but also discovering possible counterarguments to their topic.

ACTIVITY 4:
Audience Aspects

This strategy is a way to get students thinking about the importance of audience in their writing; it also focuses them on structuring and sequencing their writing projects appropriately.

Writing for a specific audience is a challenging skill and it requires writers to carefully consider their language choices in order to effectively communicate with their audience. This strategy provides an engaging and meaningful way to communicate the importance of this skill to students.

Teacher instructions

Working in small groups, students are to write a guide to their hometown (this could also apply to their school, sporting club or any shared space that's familiar and important to them), which is intended to persuade an audience of their peers from another region (state, school or country) to visit.

Student instructions

1. Spend some time brainstorming and researching the most important and interesting aspects of your hometown. Consider: landmarks, activities, areas of cultural and historical significance.
2. In your small group, discuss and decide the most interesting and attractive aspects of your location. Consider the perspective of a visitor to your town.
3. Each group member will be assigned one aspect of the town to write on.

4. For each aspect of your town, write a short paragraph with appropriate language choices for your intended audience. Your aim should be to get them to visit this aspect.
5. Organise and sequence your group's paragraphs so they appeal to your intended audience.
6. Write up your completed paragraph into a cohesive document.
7. Discuss with your class why you chose those aspects, and how you wrote about them to appeal to your audience.

Example

Our group was assigned an older audience, particularly parents. As a group, we decided to focus on the cultural and historical significance of the town of Ballarat in Victoria. We chose three main aspects to write about: the Art Gallery of Ballarat, Ballarat Wildlife Park and Ballarat Botanical Gardens. Our thinking behind these three choices was that we thought about what activities parents might wish to take their children to while visiting Ballarat. We chose activities that were cheap or free.

First, we wrote about the Art Gallery of Ballarat, which offers a wide range of artworks from local and international audiences to enjoy. The gallery is a great way to learn more about the art scene in Ballarat and spend a leisurely afternoon.

Next, we wrote about Ballarat Wildlife Park, which is home to a variety of native Australian animals and is a great place to take kids. The park is committed to conservation and education. Kids will be able to see some native wildlife roaming freely, making this an enjoyable and enriching experience.

Finally, we wrote about Ballarat Botanical Gardens, which provide a peaceful setting for lunch. The gardens host a range of events throughout the year, making them a great destination for a family day out.

> *We organised our pamphlet in this order because we wanted to highlight the attractions that would appeal to parents. We started with the art gallery, which is a cultural attraction and cheap for a family to visit. Next, we chose the wildlife park because kids would probably be bored by the art after a while, and this would give them something exciting to visit. Finally, we chose the botanical gardens because it's a good place for the family to eat, and it's free to visit.*

Reflect

This activity offers students the chance to reflect on what audiences consider the most important, and then to organise their work appropriately.

Extend

- There's also scope here to have different groups working on different audiences.
- This strategy could also work with different genres. Students could be given a prompt and have to write it into a comedy, gothic, science fiction, etc.
- There's scope here to have students include visuals and graphics, again as a focus for appealing to their intended audience.

Chapter 2: Exploration

In this second stage of the Writing Cycle, students are presented with multiple examples of texts in the styles, forms and genres they are expected to write in. We call these *mentor texts*, and they can range from fiction to nonfiction, short form to long, extracts to full texts. Having established the *purpose* of the writing in stage one, students should be starting to form ideas about the writing they might produce. This stage provides grounding in other authors' work: inspiration, technical suggestions, and conventions and features common to the form.

Mentor texts

Mentor texts are examples of the type of writing students might ultimately create. They should be selected to demonstrate a range of styles, including diverse authors' voices. Both teachers and students can provide mentor texts. In the early days of the process, the teacher might wish to provide students with a folio of writing. As the students grow in confidence with the Writing Cycle, they should be encouraged to add their own.

Short texts and extracts from longer texts are particularly suitable. The purpose of the mentor texts is largely to provide examples of technique, style, structure and language, rather than themes, issues and ideas. While it may be useful to have a collection of thematically or generically linked texts (for example, a collection of dystopian fiction, or a collection of texts about 'justice'), it is important to stress that these elements are secondary to the writing itself.

Mentor texts might include:

- Short stories, flash and microfiction
- Poetry and song lyrics
- Blogs and online articles
- Podcasts, videos and transcripts
- Speeches and presentations
- News articles, editorials, opinion pieces and op-eds
- Short films and other multimedia texts
- Essays, including those written by other students
- Creative nonfiction

Using mentor texts in the classroom

The activities in this chapter provide some options for using mentor texts in the classroom. As a general rule, we would approach mentor texts through guided reading and close reading activities. The kinds of activities used in *Practical Reading Strategies*, Leon's previous book, are well suited to mentor texts as they are short, engaging activities, which can be used again and again with different texts.

The point of mentor texts is to provide a clear example of the different functions and techniques of a text (Graham, 2020). Begin by selecting – or having students select – suitable texts based on the purpose, audience and context identified in stage one. These might be broad or highly specific. For example, if the purpose is 'to write a short story', then mentor texts may come in the form of any short story, flash or microfiction, or even short films and scripts. If the purpose of the writing is 'to produce an analytical response to a text' – for example, the classic essay – then mentor texts might include past student work, examples of student essays at various levels, or even examples of analytical essays written by academics, literary critics and professional authors.

Once the mentor texts have been selected, spend time exploring them with students. Through the activities in this chapter, or through other guided and close reading activities, explore the language, style, structure and techniques the authors have used to craft their texts. Remember, the emphasis is on the *craft* of writing.

By the end of this stage, students should have a stronger understanding of the requirements of the task – the purpose, audience and context – as well as a 'bag of tricks' to bring to their own writing. In the next stage, *ideas*, students will start to pull together these techniques as they head towards their own unique style and voice.

ACTIVITY 1:
Narrative and Reflective – Resonance

This activity helps students to identify resonant words. We term them 'resonant words' because they resonate with the reader. They leave an impression that helps form the narrative in the reader's mind. Resonant words are often used to create a strong emotional bond in readers and listeners, and help to convey the essence of the story.

Resonant words are key words and phrases that help to drive the narrative forward. They may include names, places, strong verbs, events or other words that give clues about the story's content and themes.

Model texts

This activity suits any set text that is being studied. Teachers could opt for a randomly selected page from the text and work through these steps as a class or could prepare certain passages in the text that are ripe for analysis.

Applications in other disciplines

This activity can be used in science and maths, especially where students are required to use subject-specific academic vocabulary in their writing. There's scope to have students identify the resonant words and then unpack their meaning, etymology and structure.

Teacher instructions

1. Discuss with the class the idea of resonant words – key words and phrases that authors use to drive a narrative.
2. Provide students with a selection of key words from the text being studied, in the exact order that they appear.
3. Have students write their own narrative using the resonant words, in the same order that they appeared.
4. Have students read their narrative and compare it to the mentor text.
5. Have students reflect on their writing and the mentor text; some possible prompts:
    a. A strong sentence that stands out for me is…
    b. This resonant word stands out because…
    c. I like how the mentor text uses… to show…
    d. Resonant words help to convey meaning by…

Student instructions

1. Discuss with your class the idea of resonant words – words that stick out while you're reading a text; something that resonates with you as the reader.
2. Your teacher will provide a selection of resonant words from the text that you're studying. These are in the order they appear in the text.
3. Using these words, write your own narrative using the provided words, in the same order that they appeared.
4. Your class will take turns reading their narrative aloud and compare theirs to the mentor text.
5. Once everyone is finished reading their narrative, reflect on your writing compared to the mentor text. Use these prompts if you need help:
    a. A strong sentence that stands out for me is…
    b. This word resonates with me because…
    c. I like how the mentor text uses… to show…
    d. Authors use resonant words to help convey meaning by…

Example

Mentor text

Not Big Brother, but close: a surveillance expert explains some of the ways we're all being watched, all the time (Bernot, 2022).

A group of researchers studied 15 months of human mobility movement data taken from 1.5 million people and concluded that just four points in space and time were sufficient to identify 95% of them, even when the data weren't of excellent quality.

That was back in 2013.

Nearly 10 years on, surveillance technologies permeate all aspects of our lives. They collect swathes of data from us in various forms, and often without us knowing.

I'm a surveillance researcher with a focus on technology governance. Here's my round-up of widespread surveillance systems I think everyone should know about.

Resonant words

group; researchers; human mobility; movement data; people; points; space; time; identify; surveillance technologies; data; researcher; technology; governance; surveillance systems

Student reflection

A group of researchers have been studying human mobility using movement data to track people through space and time. The point of this study is to identify patterns to work out how people move and interact with each other. This study focuses mainly on surveillance technologies to gather data on people.

As a researcher of these technologies, for my informative piece, I will be investigating this technology, and specifically if there is any governance for these surveillance systems.

> **Student reflection (continued)**
>
> A strong sentence that stands out for me is '15 months of human mobility data taken from 1.5 million people'. I think this because that's a lot of people and a lot of surveillance.
>
> The word 'governance' resonates with me because it got me thinking that I don't really know who's in charge of all this surveillance. I don't know what the rules are, and who makes the rules.

Reflect

This activity highlights to students the importance of word choice in their writing. There's scope here to have students go back over their previous writing projects and choose the words that resonate.

Extend

Using their own texts, from their own research or their own collections, students could read through and highlight/annotate key words that jump out at them in their reading and begin using these in their own writing.

ACTIVITY 2:
Informative and Persuasive – Cause and Effect

This activity focuses on one of the key strategies that are employed in persuasive texts: cause and effect.

Model texts

- Science textbooks
- Persuasive articles
- Transcripts of speeches

Applications in other disciplines

This activity may help science teachers with modelling reports and longer written texts in their classrooms. This may also assist English teachers with students who are crafting persuasive texts.

Teacher instructions

1. Begin by introducing the concept of cause and effect and discussing how authors use it to show relationships between events or ideas.
2. Provide students with a model text that uses cause and effect. This could be a short piece of writing or a longer piece, depending on the students and the genre.
3. Students should read through the text several times, looking for the following to guide their reading:
    a. Highlight and annotate key words that are central to the topic.
    b. Use one colour to highlight the words and phrases that are related to the causes.

c. Use another colour to highlight the words and phrases that are related to the effects.
   d. Look for repetitive words and phrases that show a connection between the cause and the effect.
   e. Look for transitional phrases and words that show how the ideas in the text develop and how they're connected.
4. Once students have completed analysing the text, lead a discussion of what students have noticed.
5. Provide students with an opportunity to practise writing with this structure by providing a prompt or allowing students to choose their own topic.

Student instructions

1. As a class, discuss why authors use cause and effect in their writing. Mainly it's to show the relationship between ideas and actions, and to make their arguments clear.
2. Read the model text/s that your teacher has provided you. Read it two or three times looking for patterns and structures. The following prompts may help you with your reading:
   a. Highlight and annotate key words that are central to the topic.
   b. Use one colour to highlight the words and phrases that are related to the causes.
   c. Use another colour to highlight the words and phrases that are related to the effects.
   d. Look for repetitive words and phrases that show a connection between the cause and the effect.
   e. Look for transitional phrases and words that show how the ideas in the text develop and how they're connected.
3. Using the prompt given to you by your teacher, or based on your current writing project, practise writing in this mode.
4. Swap with your peer and peer assess each other's work against the style guide.
5. Now that you have identified how and why authors might use this structure in their writing, you can apply it to your own writing project.

Example

The Effects of Deforestation on Climate Change

Deforestation is the removal of forests, and it can occur for various reasons, including logging, mining and agriculture. Forests play a vital role in regulating Earth's climate, and deforestation can have significant effects on the environment. In this report, we will explore the causes of deforestation and the effects it has on climate change.

There are several factors that contribute to deforestation. One major cause is the demand for timber and paper products. Trees are often clearcut to make room for new roads, buildings and other infrastructure. This type of deforestation is known as conversion deforestation.

Another cause of deforestation is the expansion of agricultural land. As the global population grows, there is an increased demand for food, leading to the conversion of forests into agricultural fields. This type of deforestation is known as agricultural expansion.

In some cases, deforestation is driven by the demand for certain products that come from forests, such as palm oil, soy and beef. These products are often grown or raised on land that was previously forested.

Deforestation has several effects on the climate, and it is a major contributor to global warming. When forests are removed, the carbon stored in the trees is released into the atmosphere, contributing to the greenhouse effect. Deforestation is responsible for approximately 10% of global greenhouse gas emissions.

In addition to releasing carbon into the atmosphere, deforestation also disrupts the water cycle and the balance of gases in the atmosphere. Trees help regulate the temperature and humidity in an area, and when they are removed, the local climate can become extreme.

Deforestation has numerous causes and can have significant effects on the climate. It is important to find ways to reduce deforestation and promote reforestation in order to mitigate the impacts on the environment and slow the process of climate change.

The Effects of Deforestation on Climate Change

Deforestation is the removal of forests, and it can occur for various reasons, including logging, mining and agriculture. Forests play a vital role in regulating Earth's climate, and deforestation can have significant effects on the environment. In this report, we will explore the causes of deforestation and the effects it has on climate change.

There are several factors that contribute to deforestation. One major cause is the demand for timber and paper products. Trees are often clearcut to make room for new roads, buildings and other infrastructure. This type of deforestation is known as conversion deforestation.

Another cause of deforestation is the expansion of agricultural land. As the global population grows, there is an increased demand for food, leading to the conversion of forests into agricultural fields. This type of deforestation is known as agricultural expansion.

In some cases, deforestation is driven by the demand for certain products that come from forests, such as palm oil, soy and beef. These products are often grown or raised on land that was previously forested.

Deforestation has several effects on the climate, and it is a major contributor to global warming. When forests are removed, the carbon stored in the trees is released into the atmosphere, contributing to the greenhouse effect. Deforestation is responsible for approximately 10% of global greenhouse gas emissions.

In addition to releasing carbon into the atmosphere, deforestation also disrupts the water cycle and the balance of gases in the atmosphere. Trees help regulate the temperature and humidity in an area, and when they are removed, the local climate can become extreme.

Deforestation has numerous causes and can have significant effects on the climate. It is important to find ways to reduce deforestation and promote reforestation in order to mitigate the impacts on the environment and slow the process of climate change.

> Summary of annotations/highlighting:
> - There are several factors
>   - contribute
>   - demand
> - Another cause…
>   - expansion
>   - conversion
> - In some cases…
>   - demand for
> - Effects…
>   - contributor
> - In addition…

Reflect

Students should reflect on how the cause/effect structure is used in the mentor texts and then consider how, or if, it might apply to their own writing project. On a larger scale, students should also be invited to consider how all forms of writing have an inherent structure and should continue to look for the markers that make up this structure.

Extend

Beyond exposing students to more model texts that employ this structure, students could create cause and effect diagrams and graphic organisers to further practise identifying the relationship between causes and effects.

ACTIVITY 3:
Informative and Argumentative
– Strong vs Weak

This activity involves comparing a strong and a weak paragraph and analysing the characteristics that make one paragraph effective and the other less so. Students will read through two paragraphs and make observations about the structure, language, tone and the overall effectiveness of the writing. This activity can be used to help students improve their writing and develop their critical thinking skills in a variety of subjects.

Model texts

- Strong and weak examples (our example uses our Year 10 analytical response to Charles Dickens' *A Christmas Carol*).
- Teachers should feel empowered to craft their own strong and weak examples.

Possible disciplines

This activity could work for a variety of disciplines, including English, Literature, worded questions in Maths, reports and source analyses in the Humanities, and scientific reports. In any subject, this activity can help students improve their writing skills by analysing the characteristics of strong and weak writing, setting goals for improvement and applying what they have learned to their own writing.

Teacher instructions

1. Ask students to brainstorm a list of characteristics that they think make a paragraph strong or effective.
2. Discuss the responses as a class and identify the key features; these could include:
    a. A clear, main idea
    b. Supporting evidence
    c. Logical structure
    d. Appropriate language
3. Provide students with two sample paragraphs and ask them to read through them carefully.
4. As they read, have them make a note of the features that stand out in each paragraph.
5. Have them compare the two paragraphs, considering the structure, language, tone and overall effectiveness of the writing.
6. Students should be highlighting and annotating as they read through the two exemplars.

Student instructions

1. Read through the two paragraphs that your teacher has provided. Pay attention to the main idea or the point that the author is trying to convey. Consider if they're responding to the essay question.
2. As you read, make note of the features that stand out to you in each paragraph. Consider the structure, the language and overall effectiveness of the writing.
    a. For the strong example, think about what makes it effective.
    b. For the weaker example, think about what it's doing well, and what you could advise to improve it.
3. Make a note of your observations and thoughts.
4. Use your observations to guide your writing as you continue working on your writing project. Aim to incorporate the features that you identified as being important in the strong paragraph and strive to include the improvements you noticed in the weak paragraph.

Example

How does Scrooge's character development reflect the key ideas of Dickens' *A Christmas Carol*?	
In Charles Dickens' *A Christmas Carol*, Ebenezer Scrooge undergoes a dramatic transformation from a cold-hearted, miserly old man to a generous and compassionate member of society. Throughout the course of the narrative, Scrooge is visited by three ghosts who show him the error of his ways and the consequences of his actions. As he sees how his greed and selfishness have affected those around him, Scrooge begins to feel remorse and starts to make amends. By the end of the story, he has become a kind and charitable person, willing to share his wealth, and promising to 'not shut out the lessons that [the Ghosts] taught him'. Through Scrooge's development, Dickens celebrates the transformative power of empathy and the importance of kindness. A key message of the text.	In *A Christmas Carol*, Scrooge changes a little bit. He starts off being mean and then he gets visited by some ghosts. After that, he's a little bit nicer and gives some money to poor people. It's not a big change, but it's something. It's okay, I guess. It's not the best character development ever, but it's not the worst either. It's just kind of there.
- Clear line of reasoning here: Scrooge transforms across the whole text. - Evidence from the text to support this point. - Quote has been 'manipulated' to suit the tense of the paragraph. Advanced. - Paragraph comes back to the author's views and values; student's interpretation is supported. - Good control of the language.	- Understands that Scrooge does change. - No evidence from the text to support this idea. - A casual tone – contractions indicate this. - Short, idea isn't developed.

Reflect

Invite students to reflect on how having a strong and a weak example side by side helps them to identify the characteristics of effective writing. Students can then consider how they might take these reflections and create their own 'checklist' of things that need to be included in effective writing.

Extend

Using their notes, have students create their own rubric for evaluating a strong paragraph by identifying the key features and developing a scale. Students can then use this rubric as a means of self-assessing their work as they craft their writing project.

ACTIVITY 4:
Persuasive – Exploring Editorials

Editorials are a great way to teach persuasive writing. They're not constrained to the style guide of the main publication, they can generally be written by anybody (though nominally they're a professional in the field) and they have strong, emotive language that is very student friendly.

The goal of this strategy is to identify the key features of published editorials and why they might be helpful (writer biography, headline, length, the audience of the newspaper/publication, if sources are cited) for this mode of writing.

I always explain to my class that it's important to read texts more than once. This usually elicits many groans from students when studying a novel, but when using editorials as mentor texts, given their length and lexical density, it's generally a lot better received.

Model texts

Most news publications have an editorial page. Generally, the more 'inflammatory' an editorial, the greater the student buy-in. Teachers should also consider using multiple editorials on the same issue to show students a breadth of writing voices.

Applications in other disciplines

While this activity focuses on editorials as a form, there's scope here to adapt these instructions for other disciplines, such as history, science, journalism and politics – any discipline where there is a divergence of opinions.

Teacher instructions

1. Source editorials from a range of publications. As mentioned above, the stronger viewpoints and more colourful language are generally favoured with students. They also offer a good talking point for audience and language choices.
2. Have students read through the editorials three times:
   a. On first reading, students should focus on understanding the overall message of the editorial and the main argument being made. They should pay attention to the tone and language used, trying to get a sense of the writer's perspective.
   b. On second reading, students should focus on identifying key words and phrases, annotating and highlighting them. They should think about the impact of these words on them as the reader, and on the intended audience of the editorial.
   c. On third reading, students should identify key claims made in the editorial and the supporting evidence provided for these claims. They should consider if the evidence is sufficient and relevant, and whether the claims are well supported.
3. After completing these three readings, have students discuss their observations and their thoughts about the editorials as a whole class, or in small groups.

Student instructions

1. Your teacher will provide you with a selection of editorials from different publications.
2. As you read through the editorials, focus on different aspects of the writing each time:
   a. On first reading, try to understand the overall message of the editorial and the main argument being made. Pay attention to the tone and the language used, and try to get a sense of the writer's perspective.
   b. On second reading, look for key words and phrases and highlight or annotate them. Think about the impact of these key words and phrases on you as the reader, and on the target audience of the editorial.
   c. On third reading, identify the key claims made in the editorial and the supporting evidence for these claims. Consider whether the evidence is sufficient and relevant, and whether the claims are well supported.
3. After completing these three readings, share your observations and thoughts about the editorials with your classmates or in a small group.

Example

Opinion: Without communities, conservation fails in eastern Himalayas (Red pandas and pangolins) | Tamang (2020)

Pangolins and red pandas are some of the most trafficked animals in the world. Both are distinctive mammals that are endemic to the eastern Himalayas, and both are threatened by a combination of geographic and socioeconomic factors fuelling illegal wildlife trafficking. This illegal trade is increasing at an alarming rate.

In 1992, Singalila wildlife sanctuary (SNP), part of the eastern Himalayas in Darjeeling, West Bengal, was declared a national park. In 1994, SNP was declared a major wild habitat for red pandas. The park encompasses the Singalila Ridge, a mountain ridge that runs from West Bengal to Sikkim in the Himalayas. To the west is the fragile, open border with Nepal.

Official figures on the number of red pandas and pangolins are not available, as SNP authorities and the Darjeeling Wildlife Division are reluctant to make the information public. But, according to media reports, the number of wild red pandas across SNP and Neora Valley National Park in Kalimpong is 40–45.

The International Union for Conservation of Nature (IUCN) lists the red panda as endangered, and India is estimated to have 5,000–6,000 red pandas in total. In 2015, an IUCN assessment said that global populations may have declined by 50% over the past 18 years, and that this decline would continue, and probably intensify, in the next 18.

In 1994, Darjeeling Zoo started a red panda conservation breeding programme. By 2003, it had 22 red pandas and decided to release two zoo-born females into the wild. Two more females were released in 2004 and a further four pandas were supposed to be released in October 2019. Despite these efforts, the red panda population in the national park shows no signs of increasing.

During my research in SNP, villagers told me that they had seen red pandas less often over the past 20 years than prior to that. In earlier times, they sometimes encountered red pandas in their neighbourhoods.

On first reading…
- The main message of the text appears to be that pangolins and red pandas are endangered animals that are heavily trafficked.
- There are no official figures, but media reports suggest that the number of wild pandas in a specific region is relatively low.
- The International Union for Conservation of Nature has listed the red panda as endangered and estimates that the population may have declined by 50% over the past 18 years.

On second reading…
- Key words and phrases include 'trafficked', 'illegal wildlife trafficking', 'endangered', 'conservation breeding programme' and 'released into the wild'.
- These phrases indicate that this is a severe problem.
- The words are strong and emphatic, indicating that the red panda may be extremely close to extinction unless something's done.

On third reading…
- The main claims made in this text are that pangolins and red pandas are threatened by illegal wildlife trafficking.
- These claims are supported by expert opinion from the International Union for Conservation of Nature.
- Claims are also supported by media claims and opinions from villagers who have observed a decline in the local red panda population.

Reflect

This strategy offers students the opportunity to reflect on editorials, and persuasive writing in general. Students should consider and reflect on:

- How a persuasive text might change when appealing to a certain audience
- How the text and focus might change when writing to an audience that is well-versed on the issue versus an audience with little knowledge of the issue
- How do specific language features operate in this regard? How can students ensure that they're using the appropriate language for the appropriate audience?

Extend

After identifying the key words, phrases and language features of the editorials, students should consider how each of these individually impacts the audience. Students could then workshop these key phrases for different audiences.

Chapter 3: Ideas

After identifying the purpose, audience and context of their writing and exploring quality writing in a similar area, students should be ready to generate ideas of their own. This third stage is often treated as the *first* stage by students, who, upon hearing the task instructions, will gallop ahead and try to generate their writing as quickly as possible. It is important that enough time is spent on stages one and two prior to students generating their ideas – what they come up with might surprise them.

The types of activities in this stage will be familiar to teachers who have used Ron Ritchhart and Project Zero's *Visible Thinking Routines* (Ritchhart & Church, 2020). Those routines, and the activities in this chapter, offer excellent guidance for the process of mind mapping, brainstorming and generating ideas. They are also more deliberate than simply asking students to come up with a 'list of ideas'. Again, the emphasis in this stage is on students coming up with something original, unique and worth writing. Idea generation comes in many forms but might include some of the note-taking and discussion from the earlier stages, as well as the recording of new ideas which might be used later (Boscolo & Gelati, 2008).

The ideas at this stage are not set in stone. Writers need to be comfortable with change and holding on too hard to any given idea might mean that they miss out on the opportunity of writing something even more powerful. Make sure that students are aware that generating and choosing ideas at this stage is still only a tentative part of the whole process. Students *may* start drafting during this stage, though it isn't compulsory, and serves mainly as a way of exploring and testing ideas rather than a commitment to a finished product.

The importance of free writing

During this stage, students should be encouraged to participate in free writing and low stakes writing tasks. These might include journaling, personal writing, reflective writing or short bursts of writing with no real purpose or structure. This approach – typical of writers' groups and creative writing courses – is simply to get the creative juices flowing. This writing doesn't need to be assessed, or even kept, but as students have grappled with the purpose and the exploration of mentor texts, they may start to crystallise some of that information into writing which later becomes their final piece.

This all requires *time*, something of a luxury in many classrooms. It is an important step that should not be skipped if we want students to improve in confidence, expression and fluency. Students need to take the time to gather their thoughts before beginning a first draft (Graham et al, 2013, p890).

The first draft

During this stage, students might begin their first draft. It can be incredibly rough, more like a set of notes and sketches than a final product. Students may wish to draft multiple short vignettes for a piece of fiction, or test out different topics for an analytical response. Students should be encouraged to keep all of their draft work – even if it doesn't end up in the final piece, it may make for useful materials for a later reflection or another task.

ACTIVITY 1:
Freewriting Frenzy

This freewriting frenzy activity is based on the Generate-Sort-Connect-Elaborate thinking routine, which helps students delve into the big ideas of a text or topic. The Write, Organise, Link, Expand phases of this activity are designed to help students brainstorm, write and think more deeply about their topics.

In the first step, students should engage in freewriting and write down as many ideas as they can think of. Step two involves organising these ideas into groups or links. By doing this, students can begin to see a picture forming of their topic. In step four, students can delve deeper into their topic by conducting research, finding mentor texts and deepening their knowledge of the topic.

Teacher instructions

These instructions outline a four-step process for brainstorming and organising ideas around a specific topic.

1. **Write:** In this step, students are encouraged to write down as many ideas as they can about the topic. This is a 'brain dump' phase where students shouldn't worry about the quality or relevance of their ideas, but rather focus on generating as many ideas as possible.
2. **Organise:** Once students have written as many ideas as they can, they should then group these ideas into similar categories such as ideas, themes, characters or settings. This can be done through colour-coding similar categories or by organising the ideas into a chart or graphic.
3. **Link:** After all the ideas have been categorised, students should consider why they placed certain ideas together in the same

category. They critically engage with their ideas and consider why they placed them in the same category. These prompts may help:
   a. Why did I categorise these ideas together?
   b. What connections or themes do these ideas share?
   c. How do these ideas fit together in the broader context of the topic?
   d. Are there any gaps or missing pieces in my organisation?
   e. How might these ideas fit into a larger argument or story?
4. **Expand:** In the final step, students should explore their ideas and organisation in more depth. This could involve adding more layers and ideas or conducting further research into their ideas. For example, students might consider who is involved in their ideas, who has written on these ideas in the past and what mentor texts they can include.

Student instructions

Write
- Come up with as many ideas as you can about your topic.
- Work with your friends as well – what ideas do they have about your topic?

Organise
- Look at all your ideas.
- Organise them into similar categories.
- Use a highlighter to colour-code your ideas.

Link
- Your colour-coding should help you link all your ideas together.
- Your should have a fuller picture of your topic now.

Expand
- Conduct further research on your topics.
- Consider any authors that have written on your topic.
- Use these as models for your writing project.

Example

This example was transcribed from one of our Year 7 English classes. It was originally handwritten. This student was preparing a persuasive speech on whether or not Australia should adopt a four-day school week. They were given 10 minutes to write.

Write:

Some people argue that it would be a good idea to have a shorter school week. On the other side, others argue that a four-day school week would not be a good idea. They might say that it would give students extra time to rest, do homework and participate in more sport. They might say that it would be difficult to fit all of the necessary work into just 4 days, and that school days would have to be longer as a result. It could also be better for teachers, who could use the extra day to plan lessons and have more time off to rest and prepare for the shorter week. This could be tiring for students and teachers. Some students might feel safer being at school rather than at home during the week, and working parents might have to find care for their younger children while they're at work. It is possible that a four-day school week might not actually lead to improved grades or that it could force changes on other schools.

Organise:

Benefits:
- Extra time to rest
- More time do homework
- More time for sport and other activities
- Teachers have more planning time
- Teachers have more time to rest

Challenges:
- Can't fit all the work in four days
- School days might have to be longer
- Longer days = more tired students and teachers
- Students feel safe at school
- Parents might not get day care
- Four days might not help with marks

Expand (after some conferencing with teacher):

Academic considerations:
- Difficult to fit in all work into four days
- Longer school days
- Might lead to improved grades

Logistical considerations:
- Changes school's holiday schedule?
- Some students feel safer at school
- Parents can't find babysitters
- May force changes in other areas (workplaces for parents)

Personal/social considerations:
- More rest
- More time to do homework
- Time for sport
- Teachers have more time off
- Teachers have more time to plan
- More time with family and friends

Reflect

This activity invites students to reflect on their brainstorming and organisation processes. Students should be invited to keep a journal of their work in this regard, so they can go back to it and use these ideas and strategies for their next writing project, regardless of the subject.

Extend

This activity could be extended by having students work in small groups to brainstorm and organise ideas on the same issue, but different sides. Students could also brainstorm and organise ideas for different audiences for the same issue.

ACTIVITY 2:
The Writing Rush

This activity is about getting students to write down their ideas on paper, quickly. Some students respond to the competition-like nature of this activity. They feel the pressure, so to speak, and get their ideas down. Which is what we want at this stage of the Writing Cycle.

There's a lot of leeway here for teachers, in terms of prompts and stimuli. Teachers can offer a prompt (a question on the board, an image, a drawing) and then time students to respond to the prompt as best they can. There are also plenty of websites, publications and products that offer such prompts. One favourite of ours is the *New York Times* writing prompts page (www.nytimes.com/spotlight/learning-writing-prompts), which offers a range of visual and written prompts.

Teacher instructions

1. Choose a prompt or topic for students to write about. This can be a general topic, such as 'what did you do on the weekend?' or a more specific prompt. Perhaps something tied to the writing project: 'write for an audience of scientists'.
2. Explain to students that they will be writing on this topic for five minutes, nonstop. The focus of this activity is getting as many ideas on the page as possible, not on the grammar, spelling and punctuation.
3. Set a timer for five minutes and get the students going.
4. When the timer goes off, have students put their pens down and turn their papers over.
5. Allow students a one-minute break.
6. Once the minute is over, students are to flip their paper back over and read over what they've done.

7. Start the timer again and have students complete another five minutes of nonstop writing.
8. Repeat this process as many times as desired.

Student instructions

1. You will be given a prompt to write about by your teacher. This may be something general, or it may be something that's closely related to your writing project.
2. The focus of this activity is to write as many ideas as you can that relate to your prompt. Don't focus on spelling, punctuation or grammar. Just go ham on the writing.
3. Your teacher will set a timer for five minutes. Once you get the signal, begin writing. Don't stop until the teacher tells you to. Your pen should not leave the paper.
4. When the timer goes off, put your pen down and turn over your piece of paper.
5. Take a minute – an actual minute – to clear your head.
6. When given the signal, turn your paper over, read what you've written and then, when told to, commence writing for another five minutes. Add to your ideas or add new ones that come to mind.
7. Repeat this activity as many times as needed.

Example

This example is taken from one of our Year 8 English classes. After unpacking the conventions of the dystopian genre, they were prompted to choose one and write as much as they could. This would then form the basis of their own dystopian narrative.

> People gather together and put their names in a bucket and then someone gets picked and they get killed. When the switch gets flicked they die. 30 people died. All in June. No one knows who's going to leave. No one knows when it'll be their Last word. Their Last Step. Their Last Minute. Their Last day.

Reflect

This activity gives students the opportunity to free write, but with a little added pressure. By racing against the clock to get their ideas on the page, students feel a sense of competition and are compelled to write as much as they can. The supportive writing environment is important here. Students should feel safe enough to write about whatever pops into their head, no matter how 'off topic' it may feel to us as teachers.

Extend

This activity works as a 'pass around' when the class is working on the same topic. When students have finished the first five minutes, they pass their writing to the next student, and they pick up where the previous student left off. This provides an opportunity for all students to glean different ideas and different writing styles.

ACTIVITY 3:
Idea Incubator

The idea incubator is about finding time and space for brainstorming. Often, we're hindered by the time constraints imposed on us, and perhaps even the location we're working in. This strategy encourages teachers and students to dedicate time to brainstorming and finding space to do it.

Teacher instructions

1. Set aside dedicated class time for brainstorming. A change of setting may also help. Consider sending students outside (weather permitting) or to the library. Perhaps a walk to the local park or lake. Change is as good as a holiday, after all.
   a. Students will need something to write with and on.
2. Ask students to write down any ideas that come to mind, no matter how silly or absurd they may seem. Editing and filtering are covered at different times in this book, so allow students the time and space to wander in their thoughts.
3. Once students have a list of ideas, ask them to take a step back and look for common themes and connections. This will help them to identify the core concepts they've written.
4. For each core concept, students write a sentence that summarises the idea and explains what makes it interesting or unique. This will help students develop a clear focus for their writing.
5. Using these summary sentences, students can then begin developing a more detailed outline of their writing project.
6. As students continue to develop their outline, they should remain open to making changes and adjustments. This strategy, as opposed to freewriting frenzy, is a little freer form and flexible.
7. Finally, students should take the outline they've generated through the idea incubator and refer to it while they're working on their project.

Student instructions

The idea incubator is a strategy to help you generate new ideas for your writing, and then turn them into core concepts; ultimately helping you form an outline of your project.

1. Use the dedicated brainstorming time your teacher has given you. Write down as many ideas as come into your mind. Nothing's too silly or absurd.
2. Once you have a list of ideas, look for common themes or connections. This will help you identify any core concepts in your work – this will form the basis of your outline.
3. For each core concept, write a few sentences that summarise the idea. What makes it interesting or unique? Have you got any further questions about these ideas?
4. Using these summary sentences as a starting point, begin forming an outline of your work.
5. Use this outline as a guide for your writing. Constantly refer to it to make sure you're capturing all your thinking.

Example

This example is reproduced with permission from a senior student. In place of writing, they wanted to draw a possible setting for their narrative. Annotations are visible on the outside of their drawing.

Reflect

The idea incubator allows for a dedicated brainstorming time and space – something that's important for our students. The change of scenery, and the act of simply walking, allows students to gain inspiration for their writing projects. There's also an element of positive student wellbeing in this strategy as well. Moving out beyond the four walls of the classroom will be a healthy and welcome respite for our students and ourselves.

Extend

This strategy could be extended into a permanent Ideas Intersection – a dedicated space in the classroom where students can meet and generate, test and discuss ideas for future writing projects. The opportunity to conference with teachers in this space should be given preference as well.

ACTIVITY 4:
The First Draft –
Write it How You Say it

The hardest thing our students face when writing is getting all the ideas swirling around in their heads onto the page. We've spent countless hours listening to the great ideas our students have for narratives, persuasive topics and analytical essays, only to have them *not* use them in their writing. This activity is basic in concept, but difficult for our students to grasp: 'write it how you say it!'

We've tasked our students with writing their ideas exactly how they said it countless times. The response 99% of the time is, "but it doesn't sound smart", or "but the teacher won't like it". And here's where the Writing Cycle comes into its own. Students need to understand that writing is a process. It takes time.

Ben's favourite maxim when at this stage of the cycle is 'write drunk; edit sober'. While this quote is probably misattributed to Ernest Hemingway, the underlying message is salient for first draft writing: write out everything that's in your head onto the page. A few days later, pick up the project again and cast clear eyes over it, keeping what's useful and cutting what's not. It's probably not an expression to use with students, though...

Teacher instructions

These instructions outline how to focus on conferencing with students and engaging in a dialogue about their ideas. Conferencing is a powerful tool for the writing process, and it underpins this activity for students. For more on conferencing, see the *Skills* chapter.

1. During the conferencing stage, teachers should ask questions and provide feedback to students, so they can clarify and expand on their ideas. This can be especially helpful for students who are struggling to generate ideas, or who need extra support in organising their thinking.
2. Once students have had the opportunity to discuss their ideas with their teacher, the next step is to have students write these ideas exactly how they said it. This means that students should focus on getting their ideas down on paper in their raw and unedited form.

Overall, the goal of this strategy is to help students generate and develop their ideas through conferencing.

Student instructions

To complete this activity, follow these steps:

1. After conferencing with your teacher and discussing ideas for your writing project, pick up a pen and paper, or your computer.
2. Begin writing down your ideas as you would say them out loud.
3. Don't worry about spelling, punctuation or syntax at this stage. The goal is to just get your ideas down on paper.
4. Write as quickly as possible, without pausing to think too much about what you're writing.
5. When you're done, you'll have a rough draft (perhaps very rough) of your ideas. You can then go back and edit for spelling, punctuation and syntax.

Remember, the point of this activity is to get your ideas down on the page. Don't make everything perfect at this stage – there's plenty of time for that later on. Just focus on writing it how you'd say it.

Example

This example is from a Year 10 student. The class was completing their novel study on Charles Dickens' *A Christmas Carol*. The summative assessment was an analytical response essay.

> I believe that social criticism plays a major role in A Christmas Carol because of how charles dickens wrote about the character Scrooge because he hated capitalism, Charles Dickens shows this in his text by how charles dickens makes Bob cratchit and the other workers work on Christmas. Dickens' suggests that it's not too late to learn from one's mistakes and change their ways.
>
> Scrooge at the beginning doesn't care for others. But towards the end of the novel after Scrooge has been visited by the ghosts of Christmas. He realises that no one likes him, so he decides to share his wealth with the people around him, he gives his workers higher pay and shouts everyone a christmas feast.
>
> Dickens rejects the notion of greed. We know this because Scrooge is greedy and we don't like him as readers. Greed was everywhere during the Industrial Revolution. People wanted more and more money.

This student wrote this response in their own language and in their own way. There are clearly some issues here, but there are also the beginnings of an analytical essay.

Reflect

Breaking down the hesitancy of students to write how they speak, as the beginnings of their writing journey, relies heavily on a strong student-teacher relationship. As we've written throughout this book, creating a safe and supportive environment for students to throw their ideas around, without fear of 'being marked down' or ridicule, is integral to the Writing Cycle.

Extend

As we have stressed throughout this book, writing isn't done in isolation. There's scope here to have students read their work to their peers, or in small groups to gain further feedback. Students should also be encouraged to keep notes of their conferencing sessions with teacher and their peers, so they can refer back to them as they continue with their writing project.

Chapter 4: Skills

By the time students have generated some initial ideas and started to draft their writing, they should be encouraged to identify gaps in their skills that will need addressing before moving forwards.

The skills required for writing are diverse and will vary greatly from one student to another. For example, students might need to work on technique (including vocabulary, sentence construction or punctuation), or their control of form and genre (conventions, generic themes, etc), or perhaps a further refinement of their ideas and research.

Because each student's needs will be unique, this part of the cycle requires a different mode of teaching than the traditional teacher-centric model. This is why in stage four of the cycle we switch to conferencing and 1:1 or small group work, allowing for more flexibility in addressing students' individual needs. This stage of the cycle is better delivered to small group, mini-lessons, or one-on-one as we focus these activities on meeting the individual student at their need.

Conferencing

For our ideas on conferencing we are indebted to the work of Cris Tovani, particularly her books *Do I Really Have to Teach Reading?* and *So, What Do They Really Know?* (Tovani, 2004; Tovani, 2011). Jennifer Serravallo's *Reading Conferences* (2015) also offers excellent practical advice on how to run a conference. We have tailored our approach to include the specific skills students may need to focus on during this stage of the Writing Cycle.

The conferencing period might last for several lessons, particularly with a larger class. It can be an incredibly rewarding process both in terms of writing instruction and in building relationships with students. If you have a Learning Support staff or Teacher's Aide, it can also be a great opportunity to involve them in the writing process either by working with small groups directly, or by working with the class while you focus your attention on a group or individual.

Conferencing involves making sure that students have work that they can complete independently while you work with small individuals and groups. This might mean they are working in a 'flipped'-style classroom, including watching videos or using digital content. They may be reviewing their model texts, refining ideas or continuing with draft work. Or they may be identifying the skills they will speak with you about, or following up on the conference session you have held with them already.

We use a workshop model to structure time for conferencing, and we've found that this model works well for lessons from 50 to 100 minutes.

The workshop model for a skills-based conferencing lesson

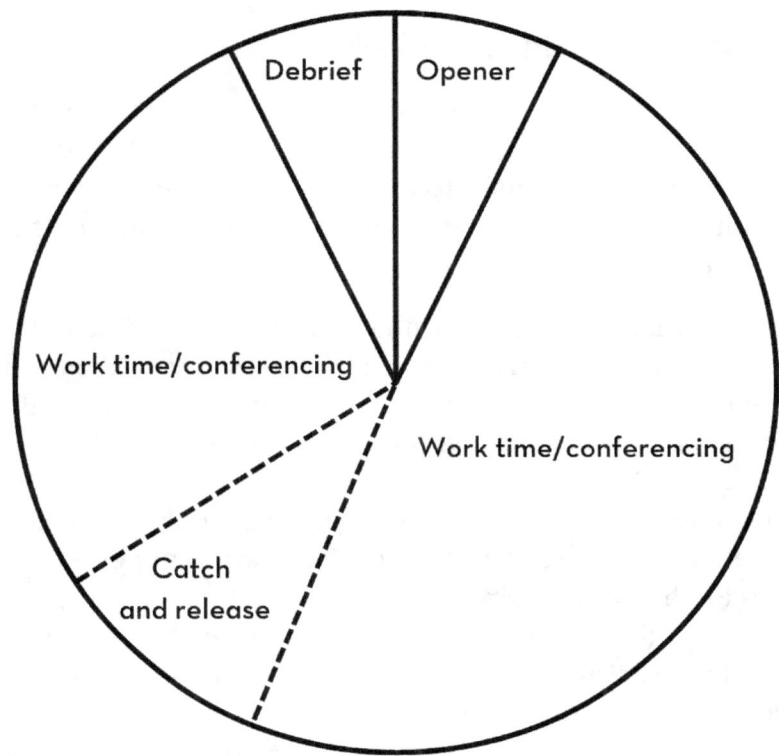

1. **Opener/mini-lesson:** The teacher provides instruction on what the students will be doing in the lesson, and how they should do it.
2. **Work time:** Students, individually or in groups, work on the tasks the teacher has set up in the first step.
3. **Conferencing:** During the work time, the teacher sits and confers with individuals and small groups. Again, the purpose here is twofold: to help the students learn, and to learn about the students. In the first round of conferencing you will be using the students' draft work and ideas to identify their skills gaps for further sessions.
4. **Catch and release:** An opportunity for the teacher to pop their head up from the conferencing and check on the whole class. This might take the form of a quick question-and-answer session, a lap of the classroom or another mini-lesson.

5. **Debrief:** A quick, five-minute discussion at the end of the lesson to check in on the general class.

Skills students might address

You'll no doubt unearth a wide variety of areas where students might benefit from extra skills work. It may be useful, after the first round of conferencing, to organise groups based on shared or overlapping areas. Some of the most common areas of need in this part of the cycle include:

- Students who need support with writing technique and basic skills, including spelling, punctuation and grammar. The grammar should be taught in the context of the mentor texts used earlier (for excellent advice on teaching grammar in context, see Derewianka & Jones, 2016).
- Students who have not fully understood or grappled with the preceding stages, particularly if they need extra support forming ideas for their own writing.
- Students who need extra help analysing the mentor texts or identifying stylistic and technical features to use in their own writing (from the *Exploration* stage).
- Students who need help working with form or genre, for example, those who wish to write in a particular form like a blog post and need assistance finding quality examples to use as models.
- Students who would benefit from strategies to plan, revise and edit their work (Graham et al, 2012, p889).
- Students who are excelling at the writing and need to be pushed further to develop their ideas and draft work.

During this part of the cycle, use successive rounds of conferencing to first identify the skills needed, and then monitor the progress of the students as they complete the kinds of activities that follow.

ACTIVITY 1:
Word Level – Error Hunt

An error hunt is a process of systematically searching for and correcting errors in the writing project. This process involves identifying any grammatical, spelling, punctuation or factual errors and implementing fixes to ensure the writing is clear.

The goal of the error hunt is to tidy up all the final bits and pieces. By taking the time to carefully review and edit their work, students will be able to ensure their writing effectively conveys the right message and avoids any misunderstandings or confusion.

As teachers, we want our students to focus on the generation and selection of ideas for their writing projects. After that, we ensure they are structured appropriately, written for the appropriate audience and convey the intended meaning. Only now do we focus on the mechanics of the language.

Teacher instructions

1. Have students print out the writing project they need to revise.
2. Supply students with a blank piece of paper. They should also have a highlighter and a pen.
3. Place the blank piece of paper over the writing project so that students can only see one line of writing at a time.
4. Have students read through each line of text and highlight any words that are misspelled or out of context.
5. Encourage students to annotate any words that sound weird or out of place. Students should also be looking for repetition.
6. As they read, students should look for any punctuation that may be missing or out of place.
7. Once done, give students time to make any necessary revisions or improvements.

Student instructions

1. Print out your writing project.
2. Grab a blank piece of paper.
3. Place the blank piece of paper over your writing project, so that you can only see one line of text at a time.
4. Read through each line of text, highlighting any words that are misspelled or out of context.
5. Pay attention to how words sound and consider if any of them seem funny or awkward.
6. Check your use of punctuation, including quotation marks for speech and direct quotes, and full stops, question marks and exclamation marks.
7. Make any necessary corrections or improvements to your writing project based on the errors and issues you identified.

Example

This example is from Year 8 English. Students were tasked with writing a creative response to Steven Spielberg's film *Ready Player One*. After unpacking the conventions of the dystopian genre, students then applied this to their own writing. This student completed their response and then went on an error hunt. The first image shows the set-up; the second shows the corrections they need to act on.

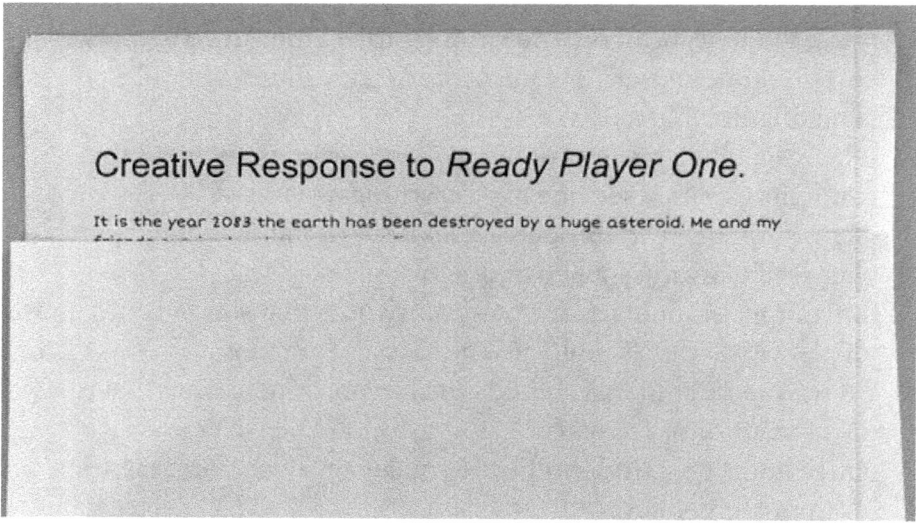

> ## Creative Response to *Ready Player One*.
>
> It is the year 2083. The earth has been destroyed by a huge asteroid. Me and my ~~—~~ *Three* friends survived underground and finally emerged to start a new life on earth. ③ days ago, me and my family were watching the news and it came up that a massive asteroid is heading to earth and will most likely wipe out everyone on earth. I *repeat*. immediately called my friends and told them to meet up before this asteroid hits earth. We all met up and one of my friends, Demi Lovato, said that we should build a base underground [and test if we could live]. None of us believed that could work but just in case we went and bought supplies and started building. Danny devito is a builder and he can borrow some machines to dig holes at his work. They start digging the whole and Danny's coworker, Dwayne the Rock Johnson, starts building the base to live in. After a day it was all done. Ariana grande and Meghan trainor were furnishing the base making it all pretty and stylish. and were also putting in food and

Reflect

While this activity is time-consuming for students, it is worthwhile. As they reveal each line of text, they can really isolate the parts that need to be worked on. And they get a feel for their own writing 'voice'.

Extend

If there is a collaborative writing classroom atmosphere, it's possible to have students swap their work with the student next to them; they work through it line by line, and then pass it onto the person next to them. These readings could be timed, and a sort of competition could be developed – who can read the most?

Practical Writing Strategies **71**

ACTIVITY 2:
Text Level – Voice Coach

Many singers begin their careers in a choir, their individual voices blending in with the others. So it is with the students in our classes. In school, our students tend to imitate the standard forms delivered by teachers. They reach for the language and the words that might make them sound 'academic' or 'professional'.

A writer's voice is like a singer's voice: unique. It is the sum of everything that goes into his or her style. A distinctive vocabulary, a preference for a particular sentence structure or it could be unique takes on issues. Ultimately, voice is the writer's personal style coming through in their writing.

Teacher instructions

1. Begin by discussing with the class what it means to have a 'writer's voice'. This is the unique perspective and style that a writer brings to their writing.
2. Read through the mentor text and discuss the style of writing. What are the features that stand out? Is it easy to read? Confusing? Any key words or phrases that stick out?
3. Encourage your students to think about their own experiences, interests and values as they begin to write.
4. Ask students to brainstorm a list of words and phrases that they feel comfortable using in their own writing. These should be words or phrases that reflect their own voice and style.
5. Encourage your students to experiment with different sentence structures and paragraph lengths as they write. Encourage them to mix up longer and shorter sentences.
6. As your students are writing, remind them to be mindful of their tone and attitude. Encourage them to be authentic and genuine in their writing, rather than trying to sound like someone else.

Student instructions

1. Discuss with the class the concept of a 'writer's voice', which is a unique perspective and style that writers bring to their writing.
2. Read through the mentor text your teacher has supplied. Identify any standout features and consider whether the text is easy or difficult to read. Pay attention to any key words or phrases. List three words that describe this writer's voice.
3. Spend a moment considering your own experiences, interests and values.
4. Brainstorm a list of words and phrases that reflect your own voice and style.
5. Consider the sentences you use in your writing – can you vary them? Experiment with structures. Does the mentor text show you a different way of writing?
6. Consider your tone and attitude as you write. Remember to be authentic and genuine in your writing – it's better than trying to sound like someone else.

Example

For this activity, we used the opening lines from Henry James's *The Turn of the Screw* as the mentor text. We chose this text because James's syntax is long and complex; he has a uniquely confusing syntax. We also chose it because it's one of Ben's favourite books.

We have collated a range of responses to the reading of the text as a class below.

> The story had held us, round the fire, sufficiently breathless, but except the obvious remark that it was gruesome, as, on Christmas Eve in an old house, a strange tale should essentially be, I remember no comment uttered till somebody happened to say that it was the only case he had met in which such a visitation had fallen on a child. The case, I may mention, was that of an apparition in just such an old house as had gathered us for the occasion—an appearance, of a dreadful kind, to a little boy sleeping in the room with his mother and waking her up in the terror of it; waking her not to dissipate his dread and soothe him to sleep again, but to encounter also, herself, before she had succeeded in doing so, the same sight that had shaken him. It was this observation that drew from Douglas—not immediately, but later in the evening— a reply that had the interesting consequence to which I call attention. Someone else told a story not particularly effective, which I saw he was not following. This I took for a sign that he had himself something to produce and that we should only have to wait. We waited in fact till two nights later; but that same evening, before we scattered, he brought out what was in his mind.

Key words and phrases/description:
- Long sentences
- The picture builds in your head as you read it
- You have to go back and read it a few times to get it
- Old language
- Complex/confusing/weird
- Dense/thick
- There's a lot of detail

Reflect

Again, this activity is a great opportunity to expose students to a range of different writing voices. There's scope here to add a bit of drama to the classroom by having students read these mentor texts in the voice they hear as they read. Students could experiment with changing the mentor text into their own unique voice.

Extend

A possible extension here would be to have students alter the perspective of their writing project – first person, second person, third person – and reflect on the impact this has had on their voice. Which did they find more comfortable/natural to write in? Why?

ACTIVITY 3:
Paragraph Level –
This Paragraph is About...

There are plenty of views and opinions on just what a paragraph is and how long it should be. Our students have certain preconceived ideas on what a paragraph should look like. Wholly, a paragraph is an idea. That idea can be expressed in one sentence, or it can be expressed in multiple, never-ending, complex sentences. Whichever form it takes, the genesis of the paragraph is the idea.

This strategy is a simple one and operates at the macro level. Simply ask your students to complete this sentence for each of their paragraphs:

This paragraph is about...

If your students answer with more than one idea, then encourage them to revisit that paragraph and simplify their writing.

Teacher instructions

1. Ask your students to complete the sentence: 'This paragraph is about...'
2. If students are responding with more than one idea, then ask them to revisit it and look at refining their writing.
3. Have students annotate each paragraph with their paragraph's idea.
    a. These annotations also come in handy for macro-level reflection.
4. Some ideas for refining and adding concision:
    a. Eliminate unnecessary or repetitive words or phrases.
    b. Combine similar ideas into a single paragraph.
    c. Supplement proper names with appropriate pronouns.

Student instructions

1. This simple exercise will help you improve your focus on the main idea in each of your paragraphs.
2. For each of your paragraphs, complete the sentence: 'This paragraph is about...'
3. As you complete the sentence, annotate each paragraph with the main idea.
4. If your paragraph is full of too many ideas, try the following to refine your writing:
   a. Remove unnecessary or repetitive words or phrases.
   b. Combine similar ideas into a single paragraph.
   c. Use pronouns to refer to proper nouns instead of repeating the proper noun repeatedly.

Example

This example overleaf is drawn from a Year 11 English comparative essay. Students were tasked with comparing Margaret Atwood's *The Handmaid's Tale* with Afonso Cuarón's *Children of Men*. This student employed this strategy and was able to shift their comparative essay from a 'block' approach to a 'weave' approach because they were able to identify and link two ideas.

Topic: Compare the ways in which The Handmaid's Tale and Children of Men show how governments control and oppress the population.

In Alfonso Cuaron's *Children of Men* and Margaret Atwood's *The Handmaid's Tale*, the government is shown to be totalitarian like in both of the narratives which are set in dystopian futures. Both texts' governments act like this because of low birth rates which lead to totalitarian governments.

In *Children of Men* the government is shown to be in control of the population and be corrupt and totalitarian by advocating for a surveillance state, the opening scene shows Theo coming out of a coffee shop and all over the buildings it encourages citizens to " report all suspicious behavior" showing that government does not have trust in the citizens and also the refugees that we learn later on are anyone from another country apart from England. The refugees are shown to be the problem and want to get into England because they have the only government still in control even though it is corrupt. This government is also shown to be totalitarian from how they put the refugees in cages, blaming them for bombings and that they abuse them and kill some of them before sending them back to refugee camps. Also how the government tries to kill and destroy any sense of hope for the people. The people in England live in fear which helps the government take control of them, the fear of the government killing them from how the refugees are treated and the fear that the world is going to end. "What do the police know about justice" this quote shows us the viewers that this is a totalitarian government and there can be no justice in this world.

Atwood's *The Handmaid's Tale* explores how the government of the Republic of Gilead is indicated to be in control and oppress the population in a totalitarian way by, the citizens having to follow a specific set of rules and there are different roles for males and females. For females they are given roles in society like wives, Handmaids, Marthas and Aunts while Males are given roles such as Commanders, Guardians, Angles. In this not so far future there are Commanders and they have Handmaids which look after their children, house and garden. There are riots and protests alot about the government and lots of people try and flee to other places. "Sometimes I think these scarves aren't sent to the Angels at all". Offred says this, showing how much she hates Gilead and how it is corrupt, telling the audience that this is not a good place to live and the government controls you from not leaving. Offred shows how the government is oppressing the population by her always longing for the past and what she had before this government became in charge and now is not a happy place to live.

In conclusion, these two stories are based on not so far away futures and are very similar in ways. Both being based on a world where the infertility rates are low leading to chaos around the world and creating these corrupted and oppressing governments. But there are differences like in children of men people are trying to get into England and the government whereas in the handmaids tale people aren't necessarily trying to get into Gilead.

Handwritten annotations:

#1 is about — control through surveillance; there's also corruption in here — make a new paragraph.

#2 is about — control through rigid rules and laws — corruption mentioned again

join these into one paragraph

make third paragraph about corruption in both texts.

> Cuarón's *Children of Men* depicts a government that is totalitarian. The UK government controls the population through the use of surveillance and fear. The opening scene shows the government encouraging citizens to report suspicious behaviour, indicating a lack of trust in the people. The government also shows its control through its treatment of refugees, whom it cages, blames for bombings, abuses, and even kills. The government's efforts to suppress hope and instill fear in the population serve to further tighten its grip on the people of England - nominally the last operating government. Likewise, Atwood's text depicts a totalitarian government that controls the population through strict rules and a rigid ranking system. Women are assigned specific roles in society, while men are given positions of power and authority. Offred, the narrator, shows how the government's oppressive rule has stripped people of their autonomy and happiness, as she longs for the freedoms of the past.
>
> In *Children of Men*, the government is shown to be corrupt in its treatment of refugees, whom it blames for bombings and abuses. The quote 'what do police know about justice', highlights the corruption and injustice present in the text. The UK government is more concerned with maintaining its power, and its borders, than with human life. Again, we see this in the Republic of Gilead, where Offred's hatred of the regime is always present, and her belief that 'these scarves aren't sent to the Angels at all.' Both texts depict governments that are corrupt and more concerned with maintaining power than serving their people.

Reflect

If students have picked up that their writing contains a lot of repetition or they are using character names over and over, a word processor is their best friend:

- Go to the 'find all' function
- Type in the repeated word
- Highlight each repetition
- Go back over each repetition and substitute appropriately

Extend

After students have identified the central idea of each of their paragraphs, they could then focus on the supporting evidence they're using. In the English classroom, there's scope here to have students mine the set text for more evidence (which all English teachers love) and work on adding complexity to their paragraphs.

ACTIVITY 4:
Text Level – Reflection

Reflective writers look for ways to improve their writing by revising and evaluating their work. This helps students not only satisfy their own writing goals, but the goals of their writing project as well. We need to be encouraging our students to engage critically with their own writing and to reflect on the purpose, audience and how they have crafted their writing.

Reflection considers the text in its entirety. What we're looking for here is not the spelling or grammar issues, but how the text reads and feels. Is the information sequenced correctly? Are the language choices appropriate for my intended audience? Is the data complete? Students need to step away from their writing and place themselves in the shoes of their audience.

Teacher instructions

1. Ask students to place themselves in the shoes of their audience. This may involve having them revert back to their notes from Activity 3: Write for the Right Crowd in Chapter 1.
2. Students will need a quiet space to read their writing aloud to themselves. This strategy also works well for partnered work.
3. As students reflect on their writing, they should be annotating and highlighting any sections they think need revision.
4. Some questions that may help students with their reflection:
    a. Does this make sense?
    b. Are the paragraphs in the right order?
    c. Am I missing sensory details, evidence from studies, quotes from characters?
    d. Is the emphasis correct?
    e. Is my language appropriate for my audience? Too complex? Too simple?

5. Allow time for students to work on their revision annotations and highlighting.
6. Repeat the process as many times as is needed.

Student instructions

1. Place yourself in the shoes of your audience.
2. If you need to, go back to your planning documents, looking at purpose and audience. Revise on what you wanted to achieve and what your audience values.
3. Read your work aloud to yourself (this may make you feel silly, but it's super valuable for picking up on your writing 'voice').
4. As you read your writing aloud, highlight and annotate anything that sounds off. Perhaps your language is too dense for your audience, you missed a word or it sounds clunky.
5. Continue reading your work, also paying attention to:
    a. Does this make sense?
    b. Are the paragraphs in the right order?
    c. Am I missing any sensory details, evidence from studies, quotes from characters?
6. Revise your highlighting and your annotation and act on them. Adjust your writing as needed.
7. Repeat this process as many times as needed. In fact, ask a friend to read your work to you.

Example

This example is a persuasive piece written by a Year 11 student. The topic is on recasting shows to make them more 'woke'. The student spent a great deal of time researching and finding quotes from actors, and then wrote this out as a first draft.

Hello respected writers, entertainment ceo's and/or representatives, my name is _____ and i am here to talk about reboots, perticarly the drastic changes made to our once beloved shows, for example the new scooby doo being writen by mindy kaling, the new Ben 10, wrote by man of action, and many other once beloved shows whos reputation has been dragged through the mud due to their reboots, being changed into political pieces. The problem is not with the reboots them selves but how they have been changed to be almost completely different shows, thus loosing the things that made them great. The latest case of this being Mindy kaling's Scooby Doo, having outraged fans by telling them the changes she has made. Pointlessly changing characters ethnicities, personalities and chore aspects of the characters all just to appear to be more diverse and not including the main character Scooby Soo himself. The HBO MAX original Scooby Doo roboot/spin off "Velma", is ment to be a dark gritty show for the older generation that grew up watching Scooby Doo, but instead of appealing tp the nostalgia of this, the writers have race swapped the characters, changed names (mainly Shaggy being called his real name (Norville)) and not included Scooby Doo, Mindy Kalling states this is because she wants the the main focus to be Velma who she has changed to her her own race and is voicing, which could be seen her to be doing for personal benefit. Whilst the controversy of Shaggy or Norville, who has been changed to african american, is he is classicly seen to be a stoner that eats a lot, although never actually seen using drugs, but with this being an adult animation and weed being mostly legal in America now, this could cause contreversy. During inerviews of the release of the Scooby Doo live action movie Sarah Michele Gellar says what she thought made Scooby Doo great quote "Scooby Doo was so much more then every cartoon, it was so ahead of its time, and it wasn't gender specific' and Freddie Prinze jr said quote" it was a talking dog, there wasn't anything cooler then that". Which i think is just a small piece of what everybody thought about this show. In saying all this the problem is not with their being deverse shows, the problem is when they take charcters and completely change them changing what made the show so great, so the writers themselves seem more politically correct.

So let me aks you this What makes it appropriate to take a childrens show and poltizize it, turning it into a political statement, instead of a source of entertainment. I dont wont want my kids one day watching a political mess, a shadow of what a great show once was.

I think if writers want to add more variety to their reboots they should simply introduce new characters which always gives them a way out if they dont work, instead of completely changing the old ones adn the show in the prosses.

i think It comes to a point where the writer need to ask themselves if they are writing a once beloved show for the new generation or a completely new one.

There are many other shows this has happened to and it needs to be stopped or be policed.

Hello respected writers, entertainment CEOs, and representatives,

My name is _____ and I am here to talk about reboots, particularly the drastic changes made to our once beloved shows. For example, the new Scooby Doo being written by Mindy Kaling and the new Ben 10 written by Man of Action. Many other once beloved shows have had their reputation dragged through the mud due to their reboots being changed into political pieces.

The problem is not with the reboots themselves, but how they have been changed to be almost completely different shows, thus losing the things that made them great. The latest case of this is Mindy Kaling's Scooby Doo, which has outraged fans by telling them about the changes she has made. These changes include pointlessly changing the characters' ethnicities, personalities, and core aspects of the characters, all just to appear more diverse, and not even including the main character, Scooby Doo, himself.

The HBO MAX original Scooby Doo reboot/spin off "Velma" is meant to be a dark, gritty show for the older generation that grew up watching Scooby Doo. However, instead of appealing to the nostalgia of this, the writers have race-swapped the characters, changed names (mainly Shaggy being called his real name, Norville), and not even included Scooby Doo. Mindy Kaling states that this is because she wants the main focus to be Velma, who she has changed to her own race and is voicing, which could be seen as a move for personal benefit.

The controversy surrounding Shaggy/Norville, who has been changed to African American, is that he is classically seen as a stoner who eats a lot, although he is never actually seen using drugs. However, with this being an adult animation and weed being mostly legal in America now, this could cause controversy. During interviews for the release of the Scooby Doo live action movie, Sarah Michelle Gellar said what she thought made Scooby Doo great: "Scooby Doo was so much more than every cartoon. It was so ahead of its time, and it wasn't gender-specific." Freddie Prinze Jr. said, "It was a talking dog. There wasn't anything cooler than that." I think this is just a small piece of what everyone thought about this show.

In saying all this, the problem is not with there being diverse shows. The problem is when writers take characters and completely change them, changing what made the show so great, just so the writers themselves seem more politically correct.

So let me ask you this: what makes it appropriate to take a children's show and politicize it, turning it into a political statement instead of a source of entertainment? I don't want my kids one day watching a political mess, a shadow of what a great show once was.

I think if writers want to add more variety to their reboots, they should simply introduce new characters, which always gives them a way out if they don't work, instead of completely changing the old ones and the show in the process. It comes to a point where the writer needs to ask themselves if they are writing a once beloved show for the new generation or a completely new one. There are many other shows this has happened to, and it needs to be stopped or policed.

Reflect

It's not always easy for a student to step outside of their work or assume the position of the audience. One way that may alleviate some stress with this process, and to add a bit of fun to your lesson, is to have students create 'glasses' out of pipe cleaners. With their pipe cleaner glasses on, students can now physically place themselves in the shoes of the audience and read through their lens.

Extend

A possible extension here is the Author's Chair. This involves the student sitting in front of the class, or a small group, and reading sections of their writing project aloud. The group actively listens and engages Ron Berger's 'Critique' method:

- **Be specific:** Focus on the big picture elements – how the text flows; signposting; language as appropriate for the intended audience.
- **Be kind:** Focus on the positive aspects of the student's writing.
- **Be helpful:** Offer suggestions about where the student can improve.

Chapter 5: Collaboration

Writing is a 'social activity' (Graham, 2018). Whether it means collaboration with another author, or collaboration with an editorial team, genuine writing is rarely done in isolation. Because the emphasis of this Writing Cycle is on producing authentic work, students will need to collaborate at some point, either with the teacher, with each other or with a third party.

Collaboration comes in many forms. At this stage of the cycle, students should have a rough draft of their writing, which is ready for peer review and editing. This can be a daunting prospect for any writer. There must be a strong and healthy culture of respect, critical engagement and trust in the classroom to collaborate effectively. Effective collaboration requires a flexible range of skills and is worth spending time on.

These activities can range from very low stakes to more involved processes, up to full editorial reviews of one another's work. The teacher can also be a collaborator at this point, assisting in refining drafts and supporting students to produce their best writing. Increasingly, students can also collaborate with non-human 'co-authors', including artificial intelligence (AI) writing apps and 'spinners' – apps which paraphrase any text that is dropped into them. These technologies are already out there, and your students are likely using them. Rather than policing the technologies, we suggest finding ways to work with them ethically and appropriately, just like you would a human co-author. We discuss these technologies in more detail in Chapter 12.

Types of collaboration

The activities in this chapter cover a range of collaborative options. Here are some of the ways you may wish to explore collaboration in this stage of the Writing Cycle:

- Group discussions reflecting on the mentor texts and ideas that have been studied so far. These discussions may help students who have yet to write a draft to move more quickly through the *Ideas* stage.
- Grouped workshops on the skills identified in the previous stage.
- Writers' workshops such as the one explained in Activity 1.
- Collaboration with an AI writing app, such as the one explained in Activity 4.
- Peer assessment, including informal oral feedback, group feedback and written editorial feedback.
- Collaborating through dialogue, explained in Activity 2.

Because collaboration requires such a trusting environment, it may be worth considering using short starter activities each lesson to 'break the ice', particularly if students are unaccustomed to working together. These can be effective from junior years right the way through to senior school.

Collaboration has the added effect of helping students who might, for whatever reason, struggle with the complexities of writing. Well-chosen collaborative activities can allow students to work with peers at differing ability levels, and with diverse knowledge and skill backgrounds. Encouraging students to work together across a range of demographics, cultural and language backgrounds and ability levels can lead to much more stimulating and productive writing than grouping students in friendship groups or homogenous groupings of ability.

Collaborating with machines

Activity 4 in this chapter explores collaborating with AI, most notably through Large Language Models (LLMs). This is, at the time of writing, a contentious area, which warrants much more exploration. Universities and school systems are currently grappling with their rules and regulations around plagiarism in light of the fact that these increasingly sophisticated systems can mimic human-level writing. We believe that these technologies will inevitably make their way into our classrooms – if they're not there already. Therefore, it is our role to teach their ethical and appropriate use, rather than trying fruitlessly to ban or avoid them.

LLMs use enormous data sets of written text to produce a convincing replica of human language. Feed them a suitable prompt, such as 'write a short story in the style of Ernest Hemingway', and they will produce a reasonable output. They can also write in an academic style and voice appropriate to essays and more formal writing, even providing references and citations. But machine writers cannot reflect. They often fabricate information, create false references and facts, and mislead themselves by going off topic or down self-directed rabbit holes.

Because of this, students should be taught how to use these AI writers as tools rather than as a replacement for their own writing. Pulling on huge sets of real and synthetic data, AI writers have access to great repositories of writing. They may be useful in helping students to generate ideas or to translate vague ideas into something more concrete. Just like human writing, the output needs to be critiqued and edited carefully. Students who use these apps should credit them, just as they would a human co-author. We explore this more in Chapter 12.

ACTIVITY 1:
Writer's Workshop (with Post-its)

The writer's workshop (with Post-its) is a collaborative activity where students can share their writing projects and receive feedback from their peers. The goal of the workshop is to provide a supportive and collaborative space where students can develop their writing skills and improve their projects.

Teacher instructions

1. Begin by introducing the concept of the writer's workshop and explaining its purpose. Emphasise that the goal of the workshop is to provide a supportive and collaborative environment where students can share their work and get peer feedback.
2. Divide the class into small groups of three to four students each. Give each group a pad or two of Post-it notes.
3. Ask each group to choose a writing project they are currently working on (narrative, science report, persuasive speech).
4. Each student takes turns sharing their writing project with the group. As they share, the other members of the group listen actively and write four points on their Post-it notes: two strengths they identified; two improvements they suggest.
5. After each group member has finished reading, they collect their Post-it notes and read through them.
6. Allow time in the lesson for students to act on their feedback and to revise their writing project.
7. This can be repeated a few lessons later when the writing projects have been revised.
8. Encourage students to keep their Post-it notes so they can reflect on the progress they've made during their writing project.

Student instructions

1. Your teacher will divide the class into small groups of three to four students. Each group will receive one to two pads of Post-it notes.
2. Choose a writing project that you are currently working on.
3. Each group member will read their writing project to the group.
4. As each group member shares, the other group members will write down four points on their Post-it notes: two strengths from the writing project you just heard; two improvements you suggest for the writing project.
5. After everyone has presented to their group, each member collects their Post-it notes.
6. Use the feedback you received to revise and improve your writing project.
7. Keep your Post-it notes so you can reflect on your progress during your writing project.

Example

We have included overleaf, transcripts of a selection of Post-its from this activity, from various groups who completed this activity in class.

> Your essay has a good contention.
>
> You don't mention Austen's values in all of your paragraphs.
>
> More 'Austen' to quote Mr White.

> You list the arguments, some I didn't pick up on.
>
> There's no audience in your writing.

Good topic.

Good evidence.

Bit of an info dump.

Funny characters.

Was a bit boring in the middle.

Reflect

We use Post-its (because we're English teachers and we love them) because it gives the students a record of their feedback. It also gives students a space for the quieter students to offer feedback. However, if the class is small or the supports are there, it's possible to have this task as a roundtable discussion, or possibly a Socratic seminar.

Extend

After completing this activity, students could read through their feedback Post-its and then focus on one note. Students could then pair off and engage in a dialogue whereby students could drill down on particular aspects of the feedback and seek further clarification, suggestions, etc.

ACTIVITY 2:
Collaborative Conversations

As teachers, we know that writing and talking are inextricably linked. When we set our students on the Writing Cycle, it's important for us to encourage them to talk with us and their peers about their project. This is especially important if the task is complex and requires higher-order thinking.

By offering students the chance to engage in a structured dialogue around their writing, they can test ideas and clarify their thinking. This strategy is all about facilitating a structured dialogue between peers. While we have placed it here, at the beginning of the writing process, it can – and should – be used at any point throughout the writing journey.

Engaging in dialogue with students *before* the writing process helps to generate and elaborate ideas. Engaging in discussion *during* the writing process offers a chance to challenge and clarify ideas and thinking. This strategy considers 'dialogue' to be both verbal and written.

Teacher instructions

1. Assign partners to each student. This can be teacher-directed, or students can choose for themselves.
2. Have students independently design plans for the writing project.
    a. The activities above may be useful here.
3. Students swap their plans with their peers.
4. Students can annotate their partner's plans or can engage in discussion with their peers.
5. The discussion should be structured around any new insights or perspectives that each peer has drawn from their plans.
6. Each partner should be given the opportunity and time to respond (if discussing) or to take further notes about the comments and/or annotations.

Student instructions

1. Your teacher will assign you a partner for the writing project.
2. You will independently design a plan for the writing project.
   a. Refer to some of the other activities you've done while working through the Writing Cycle – they may help you!
3. Once you have completed your plan, share it with your partner.
4. Your partner will then give you feedback by annotating your plan or discussing it with you.
   a. Remember: writers are always open to feedback, so keep a cool head.
5. You should pay attention to any new insights or perspectives your partner brings up during their annotations, or your discussion.
6. Take the time to consider your partner's feedback. Ask clarifying questions if you don't get anything.
7. Once you've finished discussing the feedback, make any necessary notes and then begin adjusting your writing as needed.

Example

Below is a transcript from between two Year 10 students who were discussing a personal response essay. We have reproduced it here with their permission, which may explain why their language is a little stilted. They knew they were on stage, so to speak.

Student 1:	I think you did a good job setting up the theme of difference in your response, but you didn't relate it back to your own personal experience.
Student 2:	Yeah, that makes sense.
Student 1:	Also, a lot of your sentences are the same. Try mixing it up a bit?
Student 2:	Good idea.
Student 1:	And last, coz I feel bad now, change up the start of each of your paragraphs. They all start with 'In The Hate U Give...' try something different.
Student 2:	Thanks. Your turn now.

Reflect

- As mentioned above, this activity works equally well in the planning stage as it does in the refining stage.
- The focus here is on ensuring the students have the time and space to engage in a dialogue about their writing. Through this dialogue, students will better understand the writing process, slow down and ultimately deliver a highly refined piece of writing.

Extend

This activity will work well on a Google Doc, or other collaborative software, where students can continually engage in a dialogue with each other without the restrictions of the four walls of the classroom.

ACTIVITY 3:
Joint Venture

This strategy can be an effective way for students to learn from each other and improve their writing skills. The Helper student provides guidance and support to the Writer student, helping them to clarify their ideas and organise their thoughts. The goal is that the Writer student develops a stronger understanding of the writing process.

The teacher's role in this process is to monitor, prompt and praise students as they work through the strategy. Teachers offer praise and encouragement. This kind of collaboration fosters a sense of community among the students, which ultimately benefits their overall learning and development.

Teacher instructions

1. Assign a higher-achieving student to be the Helper and a lower-achieving student to be the Writer.
2. Provide the students with a writing task or have them work on their current writing project.
3. The Helper student should assist the Writer student with the meaning, organisation, spelling, punctuation, ideas, drafting and evaluating the final product.
4. Your role is to monitor the students' progress, prompt students when necessary and praise their efforts.
5. You should also address any concerns students may have during this process.

Student instructions

1. You and your partner will be working together on a writing task, or your current writing project.

2. One of you will be the Helper, and the other will be the Writer. The Helper's job is to assist the Writer with their writing by considering how the Writer's ideas, organisation, spelling, punctuation and structure are developing throughout the writing process.
3. The teacher will be present to monitor your progress and help as needed.
4. This collaboration will give you both the opportunity to learn from your partner and improve your writing skills.

Example

Given the dialogic nature of this activity, it's difficult to provide a final written product. But this is one of those activities that gives teachers 'light bulb' moments as they circle the room.

Some extra information for each role is included below, however:

- As the **Helper**, it is your responsibility to support the Writer by offering constructive feedback and suggestions for improvement. You should consider how the Writer's ideas are being presented and whether they are being organised effectively. Pay attention to the Writer's use of spelling, punctuation and grammar, and offer suggestions for improvement if needed. You should also consider the overall structure of the writing, including the introduction, body paragraphs and conclusion.

- As the **Writer**, it is important to listen to the feedback and suggestions from your partner and consider how they can help improve your writing. Don't be afraid to ask for clarification or further feedback if you need it. Remember, the goal of this collaboration is to learn from each other and improve your writing skills. Be open to new ideas and be willing to make revisions as needed.

Reflect

This task involves an innate knowledge of the learners in your classroom. Again, this activity would only operate to its full potential when a safe and supportive learning environment has been established.

Extend

This activity can be extended into other year levels. For example, our school runs a reading programme where Year 7 students read to Year 12 students. It's possible to use this activity as the basis of such a writing programme.

ACTIVITY 4:
"Hello, Computer"

There's plenty of debate about the use of AI in education. Many articles have been published in *The Guardian*, *The Washington Post* and in academic journals. While the debate is being pushed to the limits, our students are listening and picking up on this technology. They're beginning to use it. (Ben knows, he had a student submit a complete essay using AI – it was riddled with inaccuracies!)

We propose that we can use this technology in our writing classrooms in much the same way a maths teacher might use a calculator. There's scope here to use them as a tool to identify grammatical errors, find word substitutes and learn where to place that semicolon!

Teacher instructions

1. Discuss with students the ethics and issues with using LLMs.
2. Students will need to grasp the notion that while the language sounds real, it is not.
3. As with all steps in the Writing Cycle, model the process.

Student instructions

1. Navigate to chat.openai.com
2. Ask the bot a question relating to something you're working on in your writing project. Keep it to something functional:
   a. Can you tell me how to correct this sentence?
   b. Can you show me three alternative words for 'seek'?
   c. Does a semicolon fit in this sentence?
3. Copy the segment of text you're working on into the chat field.
4. Read through the response.

5. REMEMBER: While these bots sound like human beings and their writing reads like yours might, they're not humans. They're drawing on a vast database of language and they don't always get it right. *Read* and *re-read* what it's given you.

Example

The examples for this kind of activity are many and varied, such is the nature of this kind of technology. Instead, we offer you a screenshot of a conversation we had while developing this strategy:

 how might a student collaborate with you on a writing project?

 As a large language model trained by OpenAI, I'm not able to collaborate with anyone on a writing project. I'm just a computer program designed to assist with answering questions and providing information. If you're looking for help with a writing project, you might want to consider reaching out to a tutor or teacher who can provide personalized guidance and feedback. Alternatively, you could try working with a classmate or friend on your writing project, as collaboration can often be a helpful way to brainstorm ideas and provide each other with constructive feedback.

how might a student use you to work on a writing project?

 As a large language model trained by OpenAI, I'm not able to directly help a student work on a writing project. However, students could use me to answer specific questions they have about a writing project, such as questions about grammar, spelling, or general information on a particular topic. I can also provide general writing tips and advice, such as the importance of brainstorming and outlining before starting to write, and the value of revising and editing your work. However, keep in mind that I'm not able to provide personalized feedback on a student's specific writing project. For that, it's best to seek the help of a tutor or teacher.

 if i put a sentence in here, you could mark it for me?

 Sure, I'd be happy to help you with that. Just go ahead and type out the sentence you'd like me to mark, and I'll do my best to provide feedback. Keep in mind that I'm a large language model trained by OpenAI, so I don't have the same level of knowledge and understanding as a human tutor or teacher. I can help with basic grammar and spelling errors, but I may not be able to provide more advanced feedback on things like sentence structure, clarity, or overall organization. Here are some examples of the kinds of errors I can help with:

- Spelling errors: "The cat sat on the mat." (should be "mat")
- Basic grammar errors: "She is going to the store." (should be "She is going to the store with her friends.")
- Punctuation errors: "Let's eat Grandma!" (should be "Let's eat, Grandma!")

With that in mind, feel free to go ahead and type out the sentence you'd like me to mark, and I'll do my best to provide feedback.

This is a good example of how AI isn't all-knowing. In 'spelling errors' it lists 'mat' as incorrect and then offers a correction, also 'mat.'

Practical Writing Strategies 101

Reflect

While the debate around AI in the classroom continues, we believe there's scope with these kinds of LLMs to assist those students who may feel uncomfortable working with peers, or with teachers – or those students who the teacher simply didn't have the time to get to (we've all been there!).

Extend

While this technology is in its infancy, and its impact on education is being explored, it's difficult to add a possible extension for this activity. Essentially, we should all be 'watching this space'.

Chapter 6: Publication

In our early drafts of the Writing Cycle, we had called this stage *Submission*. The decision to rename it *Publication* was not just to highlight that a finished piece of writing can be published. It is to emphasise that all writing can be a finished, polished product that writers should be proud of. Essays can be submitted, or they can be published. The former carries with it the suggestion of academia, performance, grading. The latter suggests the sharing of an idea or the putting forth of an argument. Publication means 'to make public': this is not simply a piece designed for one person – the teacher or assessor – to provide feedback on.

This requires a shift in thinking from the simple 'submission' of writing. For the student, it means that a piece of work isn't just finished and handed in, never to be seen again. For the teacher, it means that the writing can and should live on beyond the assessment period. One of the ways we suggest this happens is through the collection of student work to use as mentor texts into the future. Now that much of the publishing done in schools is electronic, it is incredibly easy to build up a bank of student work. Once these works have been produced, it is then easy to bring them out in the future to support or inspire others. As part of the assessment and moderation process, we recommend highlighting entire written responses or extracts of writing, which can serve as mentor texts in the future.

During the *Publication* stage, students will complete the final edits of their work. However, it is important to note that the Writing *Cycle* can mean that other parts of the process are revisited before the final publication. For example, part of the final editing process may include revisiting the initial *Purpose* to ensure that the writing is on target. Students may dip back into the *Exploration* stage to see if any other mentor texts could be used for final inspiration. They may wish to explore their original *Ideas* to see how far they have come or have one final check of the *Skills* required to complete the task. And finally, there may be one last opportunity to *Collaborate* on the writing, for example, having a peer or teacher conduct a final proofread.

Any writer will tell you that the work is never really 'done'. We'd happily kick a text back and forth for weeks, checking and double-checking the writing, looking for typos, seeking out ways to tighten up the narrative. That's why editors have deadlines. At some point, you just have to hit send on the email, or upload the file, or print the manuscript, stuff it into an envelope and cross your fingers.

Publishing student work

Publishing doesn't have to be a long or costly process. While you can go to the extent of having a book printed – something which many schools do through their Parents and Friends committees, or as a fundraiser – it is just as valid to print a class anthology or put together an online collection.

Here are a few suggestions for publishing students' work:

- Compile a group of analytical essays into a literary journal. Consider writing (or having one or more students write) a foreword or introduction to the collection which contextualises the essays.
- Use a free online publishing tool like Google Sites or Wordpress to make an online anthology of writing, such as a poetry site or collection of short stories.
- Record students reading work aloud as part of a video collection or YouTube playlist.
- Create a student newspaper or magazine, particularly for opinion pieces, editorials and persuasive texts.
- Print class or year level short story anthologies. Go through an editorial process with the students to long-list and short-list successful stories for publication.
- Use PowerPoint or Google Slides to produce an anthology of short fiction such as poetry or flash fiction.
- Host a reading, with students reading to their peers, the school community and parents. This might be used in tandem with a book launch.
- Use professional self-publishing services (such as IngramSpark or Amazon) to produce and print an anthology of writing for sale. This might be a collection of writing from across year levels and could include a variety of genres, forms and curriculum areas.
- Publish 'best-practice' reports of student work for use as mentor texts in future years. Anonymise the work, and collate it into a PDF for each task (after benchmarking and moderation if it is a senior school piece).

ACTIVITY 1:
Class Anthology

A class anthology is a collection of writing pieces by members of the class. It is organised into chapters based on genre, theme, purpose or audience. By constructing a class anthology, we're providing an authentic purpose for our students' writing. Collating the work of the entire class and presenting it in a structured and organised manner, a class anthology serves as a showcase of the writing skills and creativity of our students.

By gathering students as a group and having them collaboratively write the foreword to the class anthology, this allows your class to show ownership of the work and provides another opportunity for them to reflect on their own writing journey. The class anthology is one such instance where students engage in the writing process for real-world purposes.

Teacher instructions

1. First, as a class, decide on the structure of the anthology. Will it be structured around:
    a. Genre
    b. Purpose
    c. Audience
    d. Theme
2. Explain the purpose of the foreword to the class. Again, this provides another opportunity to model high-quality forewords from other texts.
3. Divide the class into small groups and have each group work on a foreword each. Each group should include the introduction, context for the anthology and summary of the chapters and themes.
4. If groups are struggling, provide them with prompts and guidelines to get them started, in a similar vein to the *Ideas* section of the Writing Cycle.

5. Once all groups have completed their sections, have the class come together and share their group's results.
6. Select the best section/s from each group and have the class edit and revise, ordering the information and chopping and changing words as needed.
7. Finally, once the class has decided on the final version of the foreword, have all members sign their name around the text – just to add a touch of artistic flair.

Student instructions

As a class, you're going to write the foreword to the class anthology of your writing projects.

1. First, as a whole class, decide on the structure of your class's anthology. Will it be organised by genre, purpose, audience or theme? Do you have any other suggestions?
2. Your teacher will model for the class some high-quality examples of forewords from other publications. They will also walk you through the purpose of an anthology.
3. Next, you will be placed into small groups. Each group will work on a class anthology collaboratively.
4. Each group should include an overview of the anthology, an introduction, context for the anthology and a summary of the chapters and themes.
5. If you're struggling, your teacher can provide you with some prompts to get your thinking going.
6. Once all groups have completed their sections, come back together as a whole and share your group's anthology. The class will go through each anthology and choose the best bits from each one.
7. Once done, your teacher will lead you through constructing the final anthology. You'll need to offer ideas on how the anthology should read, the structure and any possible changes to the syntax.
8. Finally, the teacher will print the anthology and you'll sign your name around the edges to show your ownership and contribution to the anthology.

Example

The example provided below is from one of our Year 9 English classes. The class was exploring the crime genre and was tasked with crafting a narrative in the form of one of the crime movements explored: 19th century, cosy mysteries, hard boiled or a 21st-century true crime podcast/YouTube.

There was a range of responses from the students, and to showcase these to our community we crafted an anthology. This was done as a Google Site to ensure we could upload the YouTube and podcasts. The extract below is from a cosy mystery, which has been included in the anthology.

> On the particularly brisk eve of May the 16th 1937 in Paris, a woman by the name of Bella Ridley was seen purchasing a ticket for the 6:27pm Paris Metro. Resplendent in a light faux fur coat and ankle length frock, Miss Ridley fretted over the clock perched on the lamppost beside the platform, pacing back and forth at an ever-increasing rate. As was his job, a young Parisian porter sidled forth, to offer the distressed lady assistance with her baggage. "Pardon me, madam, but are you in need of assistance with your baggage? It looks awfully heavy for a slight lady like yourself." "No, no thank you. But is there any way to speed the unloading of this train to allow the next to arrive? I'm in an awful hurry and I can't waste much more of my precious time here."
>
> The young Parisian pulled a face of regret and solemnly stated, "I do apologise ma'am, but we cannot afford to compromise the pleasure of our client's leisure to disembark at his or her own pace for the convenience of another passenger. Your train will arrive in good time. Now if you'll excuse me, my services are not required here and so I must continue to assist our other passengers." As the Parisian sidled away, another approached having purchased his ticket.
>
> "They do dawdle awfully some days, don't they? Apologies, Miss, it is rude to speak without an introduction. My name is Edgar Knott." "Pleased to make your acquaintance, Mr Knott, I go by the name of Bella Ridley. And I must confess, I do agree with you… about them dawdling. Some of us have places to be," agreed Miss Ridley.

Reflect

Consider how many of your written outcomes could be 'anthologised'. We typically think of anthologies for fiction, especially poetry and short stories. But what other forms might be suitable to publish in this manner?

Extend

Once you have collated and published an anthology, consider the following:

- Making the anthology publicly available online (with the permission of the contributors)
- Using the anthology as part of a charitable fundraiser
- Using the anthology in future years as writing stimuli

ACTIVITY 2:
Digital Publishing House

Publishing student writing on a website like Google Sites can be a great way to showcase the skills and creativity of our students. Custom websites like Google Sites are easy to set up and have a user-friendly interface, making it simple for students and teachers to collaborate on the form and structure.

A website like Google Sites offers classes the opportunity to continually add to the writing portfolio. There's also scope to offer students the chance to showcase their writing journey from the start. Uploading the first draft and final draft, allowing for students to really see how much they've improved. Additionally, there's room to publish writing from each discipline, allowing for teachers across the school to come back to this year after year with a bank of mentor texts.

We've included the instructions for how to create a Google Site here because we come from a Google school. We've offered suggestions for different providers below, as well as links. Each site will have its own step-by-step instructions.

Teacher instructions

1. Go to www.google.com/sites and sign into your Google account.
2. Click on the 'Create' button in the top right corner of the screen.
3. Select 'Website' from the list of options.
4. Choose a template (get student input on this one!) for your site or create a custom layout.
5. On the left side of the screen, click on the 'Pages' button to add new pages to your website.
6. Type or paste in the writing you want to publish. You can also use the formatting options at the top of the page to add headings, lists and other formatting.

7. To add a page for each discipline, or to structure your site around themes, genres or purpose, click on the 'Add Page' button and repeat the process listed above.
8. To make your website public, click on the 'Publish' button in the top right corner of the screen.
9. To share your website with others, click on the 'Copy Link' button and paste the link into an email, newsletter or the school's website.

Student instructions

We've included instructions for students here, should you wish to also have students organise their own Google Sites, or a site in groups.

1. Open a web browser and go to www.google.com/sites
2. Sign into your Google account if you are not already signed in.
3. Click on the 'Create' button in the top right corner of the screen.
4. From the list of options, choose 'Website'.
5. Choose a template for your website or create a custom layout. You can ask a classmate or teacher for input on which template to use.
6. On the left side of the screen, click on the 'Pages' button to add new pages to your website.
7. Type or paste in the text you want to publish on your site. You can use the formatting options at the top of the page to add headings, lists and other formatting.
8. To add more pages to your website, click on the 'Add Page' button and repeat the steps above.
9. When you are ready to share your site with others, click on the 'Publish' button in the top right corner of the screen.
10. To share your website, click on the 'Copy Link' button and paste the link into an email, newsletter or the school's website.

Example

Links to Google Sites and other providers are listed below:

- Google Sites: www.google.com/sites
- Weebly: www.weebly.com
- Wix: www.wix.com
- WordPress: www.wordpress.com
- SharePoint: https://products.office.com/en-us/sharepoint/collaboration

Reflect

While this activity is written as a class-wide activity, it may be possible to have students create their own individual Google Site and then add their work to that progressively across the year. And for those schools that are experimenting in the Learner Profile space, this could then form a project for individual students.

Extend

If your school is using Google Classroom or Microsoft Teams, there's scope to make this a publishing house of sorts. Again, students can read through each other's work and offer reflections on the writing process.

Additionally, there are self-publishing websites out there that allow writers to publish their works for the world to read. An example of some of these sites are:

- 🖉 Commaful: www.commaful.com
- 🖉 Wattpad: www.wattpad.com/stories/wattpad
- 🖉 Booksie: www.booksie.com

(Note: Self-publishing sites like those listed above may contain sensitive topics; teachers should visit these sites to ensure they're appropriate for their classes.)

ACTIVITY 3:
Writing Competitions

There are plenty of student writing competitions out there that offer students the opportunity to showcase their writing skills and potentially win prizes. These competitions cover a range of purposes and genres, including analytical writing, creative writing and presentations. Participating in these competitions can be a great way for students to challenge themselves, gain confidence in their writing abilities and potentially have their work recognised by a large audience.

In addition to the personal rewards of participating in writing competitions, students may also have their work published in the future. Some publishing houses use submissions from student writing competitions as models for future editions of textbooks. This means that students who are selected as winners or finalists may have the opportunity to see their work in print and be used by their peers across the country.

Teacher instructions

There are plenty of options available when it comes to student writing competitions, and they're not all limited to the English classroom.

Teachers should consult with the relevant teachers' associations (VATE, MTAV, HTAV, etc) and keep an eye on newsletters that publicise when they're open, and under what conditions each competition has.

Student instructions

Submitting work to a writing competition is a great way to showcase your writing skills. It can also be an excellent way to build confidence in your writing and to get recognition for your work.

Each writing competition has its own entry requirements and procedures. Consult with your teacher about whichever competition you're interested in and work collaboratively to get your work submitted.

Example

Below are links to the some of the writing and speaking competitions that our school has participated in in the past. We've also included some public speaking links, as this book has mentioned several times: speaking and writing are linked.

- Insight Creative Writing Competition: www.insightpublications.com.au/writingcompetition-2
- Write a Book in a Day (collaborative writing competition): www.writeabookinaday.com
- VATE Creative Writing Competition: www.vate.org.au/story-miniature-2022-writing-competition
- National History Challenge: www.historychallenge.org.au
- Plain English Speaking Award: www.vcaa.vic.edu.au/news-and-events/events-and-awards/pesa/Pages/Index.aspx

(Note: These links are for the 2022 competitions. Some are also for Victoria only.)

Reflect

Whenever a writing competition has been plugged at our school, there's always a great interest from the student cohort. Teachers should be aware that at times this can be an added workload (organising forms, entries, emails, etc), but overall, it's a worthwhile exercise.

Extend

If there's a particular writing competition that fits into the class programme, teachers could use this as the assessment task and tailor their teaching to this. An example of this might be the History Challenge becoming an inquiry task that forms the basis of a term's worth of work.

ACTIVITY 4:
Literary Journal

Here's one for the senior students: literary journals. A literary journal is a collection of written works typically focused on a particular theme or topic. In our case, we focused ours on the senior English outcomes. By compiling a group of analytical essays into a literary journal, students can not only showcase their writing, but future students can also use these as mentor texts. While the texts may change, the essay will be with us for a while. So these literary journals make a great resource to call on for teachers.

Teacher instructions

1. Consider the topic of your literary journal and how you might structure it.
2. Gather a selection of essays, or other works, that fit within the scope of your literary journal. These selections should be of various abilities. For example, we wanted to show our students the full range of possible essays.
3. Organise these into a logical order. We structured ours, as mentioned above, around the outcomes of the senior English study design in Victoria, in the order in which the students would study them.
4. Consider writing a foreword for each section that contextualises the essays.
5. While editing and proofreading may be an option, we chose instead to leave the essays as they were originally written – again, to show our students an authentic student voice.
6. Printing is an option or collating them into one PDF for digital access is another.

Student instructions

As a group, we're going to put together a literary journal of essays. This will showcase all the writing you've completed over the past year and showcase your talents to fellow students and the wider school community.

1. Begin by considering the theme or focus of your literary journal.
2. Gather a selection of essays, poems or other works that fit within the scope of the literary journal.
3. Organise the words in a logical order that makes sense to your group or class.
4. As a class, write a foreword or an introduction to each section of the journal.
5. Edit and proofread the work as needed, but consider leaving some of your essays in their original form, as we want to showcase an authentic student voice.
6. Decide on the method for distributing the literary journal: digital, printed and bound, etc.

Example

Opposite is the foreword that our senior English students put together for a literary journal focusing on the VCE English study design (2017–2021). While it's not possible to show you the whole journal, we hope you enjoy the enthusiasm that our students took when writing this foreword. They were very keen to help the class of 2022 with their English studies.

> Hello future English students!
>
> We're excited to present to you our collection of essays from the past two years of senior English. These essays show our work from across all areas of study. Included are essays from *Pride and Prejudice*, *Rear Window*, *Station Eleven*, *The Dressmaker*, *The Handmaid's Tale* & *Children of Men*, and *Never Let Me Go* and *Stasiland*.
>
> The topics covered in this anthology are diverse – some we got from the past exams, some we got our teachers to give us, and some we wrote ourselves. We've tried to offer a good sample of creative, analytical, and comparative responses for you. There's stuff on character development, themes, ideas, and views and values. We hope that as you read these essays, you will be inspired with your writing (and they help with your SACs!)
>
> Best of luck with all your SACs and the exam!
>
> Class of 2020 and 2021!

Reflect

This activity provides students and teachers a chance to reflect on the year's work and on how far they've all come in their writing.

Extend

There are options here to extend this beyond one subject or discipline. Students could contribute various works from across the curriculum. It's also possible to include visual and multimodal elements in the literary journal.

Additionally, one might consider creating a marking schema or rubrics so students can assess these and critically engage with the works. These can be included within the journal, perhaps at each section, or as a supplement (which, in turn, gives you a few lessons planned).

Part II

Chapter 7: Constructing a Unit of Work

The Writing Cycle can be used in isolation as the basis for a complete unit of work, or as a much shorter activity that can be carried out as part of a larger unit. In this chapter, we'll go through two approaches for constructing a unit of work around the cycle.

Before going into the example units, however, it may be useful to consider a few guided questions for producing any unit of work. In some cases, the Writing Cycle may be useful as a complete unit. In other instances, it may function as a small part of a larger unit. It may depend on who your learners are, the intended outcomes of the unit and how you will be measuring success. Before creating the unit, ask yourself:

1. **Who are the learners?** What do they already know? How diverse are the learning needs in your classroom/cohort?
2. **What are the objectives and expected outcomes?** Are you aligning them to a specific curriculum outcome? Or to a local context? (For example, does this unit meet a specific contextual need, such as addressing a literacy gap or tying in with a community event?)

3. **How much autonomy will your students need?** Sometimes – such as when introducing new concepts – it may be useful to have a more didactic approach. At other times, a more student-centred and driven approach might be more suitable.
4. **What does a successful outcome look like?** Referring back to Chapter 6, is the outcome of this unit meant to assess knowledge or skills? Are you looking for students to demonstrate their understanding of a text, or their ability to write one?
5. **What is the best mode of assessment?** Once you've answered the above, you can decide on *how* you will measure it. A complete written text – a full essay or short story, for example – may not be appropriate for your cohort, the objectives, the level of autonomy or the success criteria. Consider multiple forms of assessment, including folios, oral assessment and multimodal assessments.

The Writing Cycle can immediately replace some of your existing units. For example, it is highly likely that you currently have units on creative writing, such as short stories or poetry, or on analytical writing such as an essay response. It is equally likely that these units are text-centred, with the creative writing based on a specific author, or the analytical in response to a particular text. Swapping those units out with the Writing Cycle removes the need for a central text in favour of the short mentor texts.

The first example opposite is ideal for introducing students to the Writing Cycle, as it steps them through each stage slowly and deliberately. It may be worth incorporating this unit into the junior years as a general introduction to writing practices. It is also worth bearing in mind that the cycle can be iterated through more than once. So, in a unit of work like the second example, a teacher may decide to take students through the cycle two to three times to continuously refine and improve their writing.

The following two examples have been developed for Years 7 and 8 junior English classes. They can, however, be easily adapted up or down through the year levels.

Example one: The Writing Cycle as an entire unit

In this first example, the Writing Cycle is used across an eight-week period to introduce the basic skills and techniques used to write well. Certain stages, such as the *Skills* stage, are given more time to allow students to work on the craft of writing. Although the example provided is for creative nonfiction (blogs), it can be used with any form of writing you would like students to learn.

In the below example, there is also no framing idea or theme. Students may write blog posts about whatever they choose, adapting their personal style from a range of examples in the *Exploration* stage. For students who need extra support, it may be worth aligning the unit with a particular idea, such as having students write travel blogs (or 'travelogs'), or blogs about a theme such as sustainability.

Learners: Year 7 students new to the Writing Cycle.

Objectives: To understand that writing is a process, and that authors need to develop specific skills and techniques to craft written texts. To understand the conventions of online texts such as blogs.

Autonomy: Modelled and guided instruction throughout most of the unit, with a gradual release of responsibility as students begin to craft their own texts.

Success: A completed blog post that obviously makes use of the conventions of the mentor text(s).

Assessment: One complete 500-word text.

Week	Focus	Content/activities
1	Introduction to the Writing Cycle and the purpose of writing *Purpose*	Brainstorming around the different purposes for writing and discussion (see Chapter 6). Overview of the Writing Cycle and brief discussion of each of the stages. Generate initial ideas for the types of writing that might be produced using the cycle. Introduce key terms related to the chosen area of study. Introduce the *Purpose* stage. Discuss blogs: audience, purpose and context.
2	*Exploration*	Introduce the *Exploration* stage. Explore mentor texts from a range of blog types such as personal interest blogs, travelogs, listicles, lifestyle blogs, sports blogs and so on. Identify the key features of blogs, creating a class list of blog-writing criteria. Use activities such as *Activity 2: Informative and Persuasive – Cause and Effect*.
3	*Ideas*	Generate ideas for the students' blog posts. Brainstorming activities as well as activities like *Activity 3: Idea Incubator*.
4	*Skills*	Skills week one: Use workshopping and conferencing techniques to identify and work on specific skills. In week one, focus on skills such as style, voice and context-related skills.
5	*Skills*	Skills week two: Use workshopping and conferencing techniques to identify and work on specific skills. In week two, focus on skills related to expression, language and technique.

6	*Collaboration*	Peer assessment, guided workshops and editing. Use activities like *Activity 1: Writer's Workshop* and *Activity 2: Collaborative Conversations.*
7	Revisit the cycle	Return to the *Purpose* stage and explore whether students have met the initial criteria established for the audience, purpose and context of their blogs. Review mentor texts, check original ideas and refine any other skills if necessary.
8	*Publication*	Final editing and proofreading prior to publication.

As you can see above, the unit of work is highly adaptable to any text type – just replace the blog-specific terms with whatever you are studying. The *Skills* stage in particular will be impacted by whatever text type you are using, as these are intended to be specific skills designed to help students craft a particular kind of text, rather than generic skills. This addresses the problems with teaching grammar out of context, for example, making all of the skills immediately relevant.

Week seven provides an opportunity to quickly revisit all of the stages of the cycle to identify if anything has been left out, moved through too quickly or needs addressing, such as the audience, purpose and context of the students' writing.

Example two: The Writing Cycle within a unit

The following example incorporates a short Writing Cycle into a larger unit of work specifically focused on short stories. The unit uses both *Practical Reading Strategies* (with activities indicated by *PRS* and the page number) and the Writing Cycle to provide students with a broad skillset to approach writing their own short stories. This is far preferable to a more traditional short story unit where students may be given the entire unit of work to draft and redraft their own stories endlessly without first exploring the form itself.

Another advantage of using the cycle in this way is that it can be embedded into multiple units of work and 'routinised'. Like Ritchhart's popular Thinking Routines, using processes that are familiar to students reduces the cognitive load and allows students to focus on the technical skills of writing (Ritchhart & Church, 2020).

As with the unit above, there is no particular genre or style in this unit of work – the focus is very broadly on short stories as a form, rather than specifically gothic stories, or science fiction, or any other genre. This also allows the teacher to select from a diverse range of authors.

Learners: Year 9 students familiar with the Writing Cycle. Diverse learning needs.

Objectives: To understand the conventions of short stories and how short story writers create compelling characters and settings. To understand the process of writing a short story.

Autonomy: Guided instruction throughout reading stages and exploration, followed by student-led creation of the written outcome.

Success: Demonstration of the understanding of short story conventions through reflections on short stories and the creation of original texts.

Assessment: One to two short stories.

Week	Focus	Content/activities
1	Introduction to short stories Making Connections and Visualising (*PRS*)	Read first story aloud and discuss the general features and conventions. Making Connections activity – how do authors create realistic characters in short stories? Use a Text Walk with examples of character establishment (*PRS*, p16). Read second story. Visualising activity – how do authors create vivid and memorable scenes in short stories? Line-by-Line Visualisation activity (*PRS*, p43).
2	Inferring (*PRS*)	Read third story or set as independent reading. Guided annotation activity. Inferring activity – Read Between the Lines (*PRS*, p79). How do authors create meaning in short stories?
3	Writing Cycle part one *Purpose, Exploration* and *Ideas*	Introduce the task to write a short story. Identify mentor texts and discuss. Complete activities such as *Activity 1: The Roadmap* and *Activity 2: Think Tank*.
4	Writing Cycle part one continued *Skills*	Use workshopping and conferencing techniques to identify and work on specific skills. In week one, focus on skills such as style, voice and context-related skills.
5	Questioning (*PRS*)	Revisit some of the mentor texts and student draft work (if it has been created). Complete Questioning activities such as Deep Questions (*PRS*, p68).

6	Writing Cycle part two *Collaboration and Publication*	Peer assessment, guided workshops and editing. Final editing and proofreading prior to publication. *Activity 3: Joint Venture* and *Activity 4: "Hello, Computer".*
7	Summarising and Synthesising (*PRS*)	Complete activities designed to summarise and synthesise the knowledge gained over the course of the unit about short stories, including reflecting on their own short stories. 10 Words or Less summary activity (*PRS*, p104).
8	*Publication*	Final editing and proofreading prior to publication.

Notes on the example units

These examples are not intended to be a complete, workable unit of work. They should, however, demonstrate how the Writing Cycle can be adapted to fit different kinds of unit. Often in schools we separate reading and writing into discrete skills. This can be useful when focusing on particular elements such as close reading techniques or the skills of crafting a particular text. However, it can also be very useful to combine the skills of reading and writing, acknowledging that they are of course two sides of the same coin.

By the end of either of these units, students should be more aware that writing is a process, and not just an outcome.

Practical strategies for this chapter

The suggestions in this chapter may not exactly fit with your cohort or context, or the amount of time you have available. Consider the following activities to help with planning writing units:

- Refer to the curriculum documents (such as ACARA, or your state curriculum). Conduct a 'gaps analysis' of writing techniques by looking for language outcomes. Map these to the *Skills* stage of the Writing Cycle in units across various year levels.
- Take a big picture view of your curriculum across all year levels. Is there a balance between reading, writing and speaking and listening?
- As a faculty, create a pool of appropriate mentor texts for all writing units across all year levels ahead of time. This will make the overall planning process much easier and will save time in the long run.
- Be flexible with unit plans. Create them on shared online documents such as in Google Workspace for Education or Microsoft Teams so that they can be adjusted and updated as needed.

Chapter 8: Giving Feedback

Inherent in the Writing Cycle is the need to move away from viewing writing as just a product, and towards respecting the whole process. This means that the assessment of writing should occur at every step of the way. Assessment can be formal or informal and should provide opportunities for ongoing feedback. It may also be useful to break longer written assessments into shorter folio pieces that target specific forms, skills or techniques.

Assessing the cycle

Each stage of the Writing Cycle can be assessed independently either through separate tasks or as a single assessment that is returned to throughout the unit of work. Your judgement of the work in each stage may come from a single activity – such as *Activity 2: The Writing Rush* from the *Ideas* stage – or through a combination of activities. Students might also self-assess at various stages throughout the cycle.

While ongoing formative assessment and feedback may seem daunting at first, it actually lightens the overall workload of marking. Rather than collecting and marking 20-something complete essays, the teacher may assess and give feedback throughout the unit, meaning that the final submitted piece requires just a grade and a summative comment. A lot of teacher time is wasted providing extensive feedback or corrections on final submissions. I'd almost guarantee that most of the comments and feedback are never read, and that students will seek out the final grade and perhaps glance at the end comment. Ongoing assessment is delivered at the point in time and place where it is most useful.

Ongoing assessment also provides more opportunities for students to demonstrate their capabilities. For various reasons, a student with great ideas and the ability to discuss and analyse texts may struggle when it comes to ultimately producing a written outcome. Ongoing assessment provides these students opportunities to succeed throughout and may also help the teacher to understand the issues faced in the final stage.

One way to assess the process is to use a rubric like the one opposite to grade each stage of the cycle. An even better suggestion would be to co-design the criteria alongside your students, asking them what they think a successful outcome might look like at each stage of the cycle. The basis for the following assessment may be a folio of items collected along the way – such as a submission of the work from the activities in this book – or by teacher judgements or student self and peer assessments throughout the unit of work.

Assessing the cycle

Stage	No evidence	Developing	Satisfactory	Above standard	Well above standard
Purpose	No evidence of understanding of purpose, audience or context	Can articulate the purpose of the writing with support	Identifies the purpose, audience and context for this writing outcome	Understands how purpose, audience and context individually and collectively impact the written outcome	Understands the nuance of purpose, audience and context and can articulate how each individually and collectively impacts the written outcome
Exploration	No evidence of engagement with the mentor texts	Is able to identify features of the mentor texts studied in class	Explores the mentor texts studied in class and is able to identify key aspects such as style, features and conventions	Explores both the mentor texts studied in class and identifies own texts for independent study	Engages with and analyses multiple mentor texts including those studied in class, and texts selected for independent study
Ideas	No evidence of the development of initial ideas	Generates at least one idea based on the purpose and mentor texts, possibly with additional support	Generates several possible ideas based on the purpose and the mentor texts studied in class	Generates several original and interesting ideas based on the purpose and the mentor texts studied in class	Generates interesting, unique and sophisticated ideas in response to the purpose and the mentor texts. Is flexible and able to adjust ideas based on requirements of the outcome
Skills	No evidence of skills development	Works on specific skills to improve writing	Responds to feedback and works to develop skills in identified areas	Seeks ways to improve and responds to feedback, working to develop skills in identified areas	Is able to identify skills required for own development and seek out ways to improve. Responds very well to feedback and shows definite growth
Collaboration	No evidence of collaboration	Acknowledges feedback from peer assessment and participates in group workshops	Works well with others including through peer assessment and workshops	Works well with others including through peer assessment and workshops. Offers and acts on feedback	Works effectively with others including through peer assessment and group workshops. Takes on leadership roles in a group and gives and receives feedback well
Publication	No final submission	Submits a final piece	Publishes a final piece which meets the expectations of the purpose, audience and context	Publishes a final piece which exceeds the expectations of the outcome	Publishes a final piece/s which exceed the expectations of the outcome. Demonstrates confidence and clarity in writing and addresses each stage of the cycle

Comparative marking

When students are encouraged to write in different forms and modes, it can be very difficult to assess the final outcome. If student A writes a blog, student B a folio of poetry and student C an essay, many teachers would find it difficult to assess these different responses against a common set of criteria. Yet, if we truly value the writing process over the product, there will be many occasions where this more flexible approach is appropriate, and where student choice should be encouraged.

While it might be more straightforward to decide that every student must write a blog post, a short story, an essay or some other common form, comparative marking can be achieved across different forms as long as the criteria is focused on shared, assessable aspects of the task. When developing comparative criteria for assessing different text types, it may be useful to ask the following questions:

- How can students change the form of the text, while keeping the same purpose, audience and elements of the context?
- Is there an 'ideal' form for the outcome of this task?
- Is it worth presenting multiple options or letting students choose from any form?
- What is being assessed, and what form(s) are the most suitable vehicle for those outcomes?
- Is a written outcome the best decision for what we want to assess? (As opposed to, for example, an oral, a discussion, a visual or multimodal text.)
- What common elements do we wish to assess that can be separated from the form?

In order to identify the common elements, return to the Writing Cycle. The obvious place to start is the purpose, audience and context. Consider the following:

Purpose: To produce a text that entertains and informs the audience about a new technological innovation.
Audience: Australian teenagers, particularly those living in metropolitan areas with access to the technology.
Context: A recent online publication.

The obvious form suggested by the above criteria might be an online article, blog or review. But to entertain and inform, a student might just as easily choose to write a creative piece, such as a short story that demonstrates the innovation, or a script for a short film that functions as an advertisement. Any of those forms can be assessed by using the common criteria of purpose, audience and context.

This is where a comparative marking rubric may prove useful (AERO, 2022, p18). The following example is again just one way to develop criteria for a written outcome. Senior English teachers in Victoria will recognise the format as similar to the expected qualities for the VCE English examination.

Comparative marking rubric example

	Marks	Content/activities
High	9–10	Demonstrates a sophisticated approach to the purpose, audience and context showing a deliberate and nuanced understanding of how form affects meaning
		Sophisticated and purposeful analysis of the mentor texts including mentor texts selected for independent study. Development of ideas and skills appropriate to the purpose and clearly based on the study of mentor texts
		Expressive, fluent and confident writing that uses skills and techniques which are clearly influenced by the mentor texts
	8	Demonstrates a clear understanding of how purpose, audience and context affects meaning
		Demonstrates an ability to analyse mentor texts, including texts selected for independent study. Development of ideas and skills appropriate to the purpose and clearly based on the study of mentor texts
		Fluent and confident writing that uses skills and techniques which are clearly influenced by the mentor texts

Medium	7	Demonstrates an understanding of how purpose, audience and context affects meaning
		Explores mentor texts, including some selected for independent study. Develops ideas and skills which are related to the purpose
		Clear and effective language that uses skills and techniques which are clearly influenced by the mentor texts
	6	Demonstrates an understanding of how purpose, audience and context affects meaning
		Explores mentor texts. Develops ideas and skills which are related to the purpose
		Clear language
	5	Demonstrates an understanding of the purpose, audience and context
		Explores mentor texts
		Clear language
	4	Demonstrates some understanding of purpose, audience and context
		Explores some of the mentor texts
		Language is mostly clear
Low	3	Demonstrates limited understanding of purpose, audience and context
		Limited use of the mentor texts for ideas
		Shows basic language control, with some use of the mentor texts for technique and style
	1–2	Demonstrates very limited understanding of purpose, audience and context
		Very limited use of the mentor texts for ideas
		Shows some language control, with limited use of the mentor texts for technique and style
	0	Shows no attempt to engage in the writing task

A process for comparative marking

Comparative marking for writing tasks is effective but takes a while to establish. It requires benchmarking and moderation processes, and an acceptance of the fact that these are not finite judgements: a 7 one year might be more like a 6 or even a 5 the next, dependent on the cohort.

The advantages of this marking process are that you quickly build a collection of benchmarked examples of student writing that can be used year after year. These benchmarks become an invaluable resource for future students and improve the overall quality of writing over time, as it makes your expectations much clearer.

Here's the process:

1. Ensure every teacher assessing the outcome is familiar with the expected qualities.
2. Collect student work for assessment. Each teacher roughly sorts their assessment pile into high, medium and low.
3. Each teacher selects one high, one medium and one low script to submit for benchmarking. For example, four teachers of Year 10 would submit a total of 16 papers to benchmark.
4. Either separately or as a group, each benchmark paper is awarded marks based on the expected qualities. Note that the qualities are not specific to a particular form, so it is possible to assess a blog versus a short story, or an essay versus a piece of flash fiction, and so on.
5. Discuss the benchmarks and agree on the final marks. These 16 papers now become the basis for the rest of the comparative marking.
6. Each teacher marks their individual pile by comparing their pieces to the benchmarks.
7. A final moderation meeting – which can be virtual and asynchronous – is held to allow teachers to double-check, clarify and question grades.

As we said, it's not an easy process. It is, however, rigorous and fair.

This style of marking relies more on a wholistic approach to the piece being assessed than a criteria-based rubric with levelled descriptors. For example, for a student to get a 7, they need to have met the expected qualities *on balance*. We don't penalise students for occasional mistakes, and we don't negatively mark – we are looking to award what's there.

Your choice

Ultimately, there are many ways to assess writing. You may choose to use a folio-based assessment with a rubric for a junior level task and a comparative assessment for senior levels. You might do it the opposite way around. You could choose to assess using a blend of the folio-based and comparative approaches, with some of the feedback and assessment carried out during the unit of work, and comparative marking used at the very end to grade the final piece.

The key is to ensure the assessment method matches the purpose of the written outcome. As we said in Chapter 6, if you're looking to assess writing for writing's sake, then focus on the skills required, and not the knowledge of the texts you have studied along the way.

Practical strategies for this chapter

Assessing writing is best approached in a team. If your school does not have multiple people teaching the same year level, then encourage teachers to form small groups to help with moderation and comparative judgement.

- *Always* save examples of student work from any final written task. Electronic submissions make this easy, but having a separate folder of high, medium and low responses should be a minimum expectation.
- In the senior years, lobby your leadership team for time to complete benchmarking and moderation. In states like Victoria, where VCE English is compulsory, you will likely have the largest cohort of students in the school and there is ample justification for the time allowance.
- Write out a faculty (or school) policy for benchmarking and moderation processes. It makes it much easier to bring new staff up to speed, and provides a point of reference when speaking with students.

Chapter 9: Writing Across the Curriculum

As with Leon's previous book, *Practical Reading Strategies*, the processes that were developed for the English classroom are applicable across all areas of the curriculum. Writing is carried out in almost every subject area, from short question responses to extensive lab reports, evaluations and analyses.

The Writing Cycle can be applied in any instance where a piece of writing is required that fits a particular style, form or purpose. Most of the activities in this book can be adapted to suit any subject area.

'We're all teachers of literacy'

Many teachers have heard the cliché 'we're all teachers of literacy'. The problem is, it's not true. In Australia, as with other countries, most initial teacher education is domain-specific, locked into a particular subject area. While many universities include units on literacy, most teachers do not train as literacy teachers – they train for Science, or Health and PE, or Humanities, or another particular domain. In a

US study of secondary teachers across the domains, Gillespie et al reported that "a majority of teachers indicated they did not receive adequate preservice or inservice preparation on how to use writing to support learning" (Gillespie et al, 2013, p1043). Even English teachers don't specifically train to teach literacy – we train largely to explore literature and the creation of texts.

Even though many of us were not trained to teach reading and writing, we all have discipline-specific language that is core to our subjects. "Disciplinary literacy… is an emphasis on the knowledge and abilities possessed by those who create, communicate and use knowledge within the disciplines" (Shanahan & Shanahan, 2012, p8).

We're not suggesting that all teachers are teachers of literacy. We do, however, think that at some point all teachers will have to teach writing. The Writing Cycle offers a way to do that which is structured, consistent across faculties and can be used by any teachers whether they have a grounding in literacy skills or not.

Writing across the curriculum

Here are a few examples of the kinds of writing a student might be required to produce in a single term:

- English – a short story
- History – a source analysis
- Geography – a case study
- Health and PE – a report
- Languages – a script for a dialogue
- Mathematics – long-worded questions
- Science – a lab report
- Visual Arts – a critique of an artwork
- Technology – a response to a client's brief
- Music – an evaluation of a performance

Each of these tasks requires a discrete set of skills and a different response from the student in terms of style, voice, register and tone. Some are formal (such as the source analysis and lab report), others less formal (the dialogue and the evaluation). Some are written for a specific audience, others are personal and reflective, and some have no clear stated audience other than the teacher/assessor.

Expecting students to create so many different forms of writing places a heavy burden on them. Using the Writing Cycle consistently across subject areas reduces that burden by making certain parts of the process predictable and consistent.

Here are some examples:

Geography case study

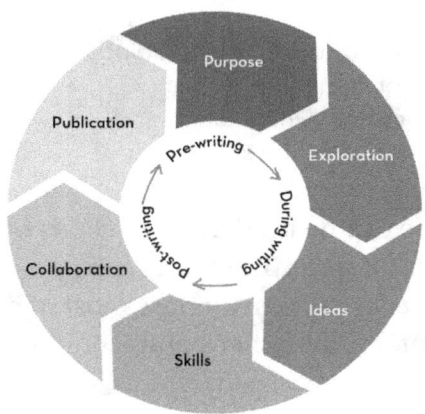

Purpose: Produce a case study on coastal erosion for a nearby coastal area for submission to the council.
Exploration: Examples of case studies from previous students and online.
Ideas: Generation of ideas for where and how to conduct the case study.
Skills: Review of skills required to complete case study, including mapping.
Collaboration: Collaboration on the process of collecting data and writing the case study.
Publication: Final editing and submission of the case study.

Music evaluation

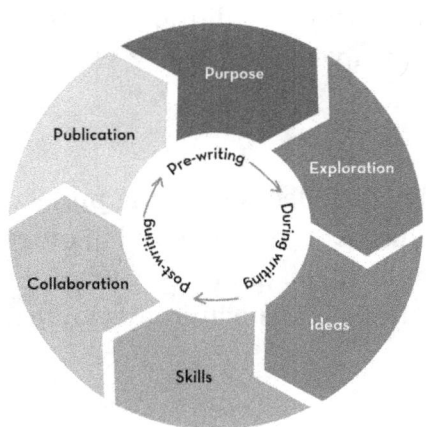

Purpose: Evaluate your performance as part of an ensemble in a personal reflection.
Exploration: Examples of evaluations written by the teacher.
Ideas: Brainstorming key points which need to be included in the evaluation.
Skills: Review of key metalanguage and terminology which must be used in the evaluation.
Collaboration: Discussion of the evaluation with other ensemble members.
Publication: Final editing and submission of the evaluation.

Languages dialogue script

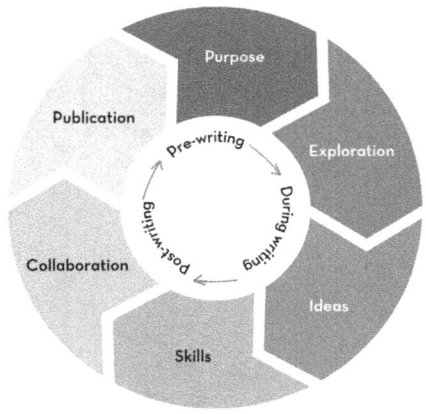

Purpose: Produce a script for a conversation between two speakers as part of your final assessment.
Exploration: Audio and transcribed conversations in topics similar to the areas covered in class.
Ideas: Brainstorming ideas for conversation.
Skills: Review of the unit's key vocabulary and language/grammar skills.
Collaboration: Practice dialogue in pairs or small groups.
Publication: Final editing and submission of the script.

As you can see above, the Writing Cycle can be used across a series of lessons, or in a relatively short amount of time. The Geography case study, for example, may take several weeks and encompass most of a unit of work. The evaluation and script, on the other hand, could be completed in one or two lessons.

Using activities across the curriculum

Many of the activities in this book can easily be adjusted for other curriculum areas. Here are a few brief examples:

Resonant words

While we have used this for a narrative or reflective writing project, this activity can be adjusted to focus on other forms required in other disciplines. A simple adjustment might be to *not* put the key words in the order they appear, but to explore these words within the context they're written.

Possible applications in other subjects include:

- Maths: identifying key words and phrases in worded questions. Applying them to student answers.
- Science: identifying the key words and phrases in journal articles or lab reports. Again, modelling how to use this language in context.
- History: reading through source analyses and identifying the key words and phrases that historians use in their writing.

Strong vs weak

This activity can work across all disciplines, effectively. Teachers should consider building up their bank of mentor texts and then deploying them in the classroom for the purposes of exploring what makes a strong response – or a weak response – in their individual disciplines.

Moreover, and this is explored in this book, teachers should model and self-edit as they do, the writing of a strong response, and a weak response. Thinking aloud as they do it. This is a powerful tool for our students' learning.

Error hunt

Some adjustments to this activity can be deployed in the History classroom or the Arts. Instead of focusing on the errors in a lengthy response, students can instead focus on how the sentences are constructed and what language is being used. This is sort of an amalgam of resonant words and strong vs weak. Call it: Vocab Hunt, or Sentence (or some other word starting with S). Either way, students can slowly unpack a mentor text and focus on the constituent parts, and then apply these to their own writing.

Voice coach

This task can be used to explore the 'voices' of academic writing. Applications exist in the Humanities, Maths, Science and the Arts. Identifying the particular voice of a written piece will aid students in completing their writing project.

Practical strategies for this chapter

If you are a Head of English, you probably have regular meetings with the other faculty leaders. Use these as an opportunity to start conversations about Writing Strategies in their domain. Think of the following as discussion prompts:

- What are the requirements for writing longer responses, if any?
- Who are the audiences and what are the purposes of these writings?
- What difficulties do students face when writing in your subject area?

Chapter 10: Being a Writer

A book on writing instruction wouldn't be complete without a chapter on actually being a writer. If we truly value the process of writing, then we have to show students that there are real-world applications of writing beyond school. Contrary to what many people believe, 'writer' really is a profession! Yet what students (and teachers) might think of as the 'job' of being an author or writer isn't necessarily the whole picture.

There is, of course, the stereotypical starving artist, hammering away at the typewriter or scrawling in countless notebooks in pursuit of the muse; the author working on their craft, trying for the piece of work that finally breaks through into something meaningful and perhaps even life changing. It's a romantic, idealised image that treats the author as both an underdog and outcast, and a celebrity and superhuman. And it's not a *particularly* helpful image for our students.

Writers come in many flavours. Like any profession, there are nuances and variations. There are roles within other occupations that require writing as a significant part of the work. We happen to think that teaching should be one of those professions, and that teachers often make excellent, compelling writers. In this chapter, we'll explore the role of teachers as writers, and offer advice for discussing writing with students as a legitimate career move.

Teachers as writers

Writing is a great creative outlet, but it also helps to sharpen your ideas around concepts and content. It can go a long way to improving feelings of self-efficacy and proficiency even in areas you may usually find out of your comfort zone. Over our years teaching – despite English being our main method – we've both taught, and written about, digital technologies, STEAM, humanities, and entrepreneurial education. Writing for or about a subject forces you to identify gaps in your knowledge and research what's missing, whether it's your main method or not.

Writing is essential to communication, and teaching is essentially all about communication. Whether it's the ability to clearly articulate an idea to a student, or crafting a carefully worded email to a parent, teachers rely on written communication skills as part of the daily job. But there are ways to extend these natural skills beyond the ordinary.

Writing in the classroom

The most obvious place to start honing your skills – and one of the most beneficial – is in the classroom. As English teachers, there are obviously times when it's useful for us to be able to model writing in various forms for students, from demonstrating how to construct a sentence through to taking a class through an entire essay or short story. Producing the writing yourself also gives you the ultimate quality control – many teachers have probably faced a situation where they're going through something written by another author, only to find that the meaning is obscured, the content isn't entirely in the right context or the quality is low.

Think about the kinds of writing your students might need to read or produce themselves. What are the specific forms of text studied in your curriculum area? One of the key principles of disciplinary literacy is the understanding that different subjects require different ways of thinking and communicating. Students need guidance in writing reports, or understanding how case studies are constructed, or in the difference between a source analysis and an argumentative essay.

Writing in the classroom also helps forge stronger relationships with your students. They need to see that writing is a messy and imperfect process. If the only text they ever see comes from a textbook – edited and proofread dozens of times before publication – then they will have a skewed version of reality, and an understandable reluctance to make mistakes. Show them your working out – go through the whole process of writing from planning through to publication, and go through the process with them, not behind closed doors.

Advice on classroom modelling

As part of the Writing Cycle, we make extensive use of modelling and mentor texts. Guided instruction and gradual release of responsibility are key to the success of the cycle, and as such, teachers need to be confident modelling writing in front of students.

We can adapt many of the activities in this book to use *teacher writing* instead of, or as well as, the mentor texts. For example, a teacher might create a unique text using a mentor text, mirroring the process they expect from their students. Or a teacher might choose to model a particular skill or technique, working through it live in front of the class.

Try incorporating some of the following into your lessons:

- Whenever you ask your students to write anything – from a short answer to a paragraph – be prepared to demonstrate some or all of the same writing on the whiteboard.
- Be critical of your own writing. Write, and then edit, in front of the class. Ask for feedback and suggestions from the students.
- Articulate the purpose, audience and context of your own writing. Play around with them as if they are variables, rewriting after changing the audience, or shifting the purpose.
- Don't take yourself too seriously! Everyone is shy about writing in front of others. Make writing a fun and engaging activity by keeping it light and inviting students to participate in co-writing in front of the class.

Writing outside the classroom

As professionals, it is also a great idea for teachers to write outside the classroom. This includes writing for journals and magazines, online articles, blog posts and even books. A lot of great ideas and activities are locked up inside teachers' minds, and writing is a great way to share that knowledge.

In a blog post in 2022, Leon wrote about his process for getting into professional writing.

> "This doesn't have to be the way you do it. You might stumble into writing accidentally, perhaps by getting asked to put some thoughts down on paper after a successful programme. You might fall into writing through your research, moving from academic writing to writing for a broader audience. You might – like me – start with a desire to write fiction, and then spend more time than you expected in nonfiction before eventually circling back. But this process worked for me, and it has worked for many other teacher-writers I've spoken with over the years."

Have a go at the following:

1. Just write. Write in bulk. Write anything. Journal, write fiction, write opinion pieces no one will ever see. Just get words down on the page.
2. Build your subject matter expertise and carve a niche. Take part in research projects, communities of practice and professional learning, and write about your reflections.
3. Publish through journals, articles and magazines. Approach publishers directly and ask if they accept teacher submissions.
4. Present. Speak at conferences for your teaching association, or education more broadly. Run professional learning seminars and workshops that reference your writing. Get noticed.
5. Publish commercially. If you're lucky enough to be approached directly, and the publisher aligns with your values, seize the opportunity to get published. If you have a great idea and a body of work – including writing and presenting – approach publishers directly.
6. Create a virtuous cycle. Write, present and then write some more.

Writing as a teacher unlocks a lot of benefits, from demonstrating your professional expertise to showing students that you really do value the writing process. If something from this book resonates with you, let us know – we're always keen to publish guest posts from other teachers!

Writing as a profession

Not all of your students will want to pursue a career in writing. It is worth demonstrating, however, that such careers are possible, and that they come in a diverse range of options. Aside from the stereotypical author, writing forms the backbone of many careers, for example:

- Professional writers, consultants and speakers in industry. Many people, when they reach a particular level in their careers, step out of the industry to help others through their writing, speaking and coaching. This was Leon's pathway after 15 years in the classroom.
- Content writers. Despite the growing use of AI in marketing and content writing (see Chapter 12), there is always going to be a demand for engaging content. Content writing spans all industries and includes marketing, online media, education and training, and more.
- Blogging and journalism. It is possible to build a career in blogging, and traditional journalism is far from dead. People will always want to read interesting material across a range of diverse and sometimes very niche subject areas. If students are passionate about something, they can make a career out of writing about it.
- Grant and application writing. There are some niche careers within the world of writing, which often get overlooked. Many Government and not-for-profit organisations have specific roles for people to write applications for grants and funding. It requires a deep knowledge of the industry and an understanding of persuasive writing and argument.
- Editors and publishers. It doesn't always have to be about your own writing. Editors and publishers work with other authors to finesse writing and get it out into the world, and are a vital part of the industry.

Showing students the possibilities makes the writing process real, and has the potential to increase both the engagement and enjoyment of learning to write.

Practical strategies for this chapter

Putting yourself out there as a writer can be daunting, but very rewarding. Try the following activities to get started:

- Review your curriculum documents, scope and sequence, and unit plans. Identify places ahead of time where you can model writing for your students.
- Devote a faculty meeting to discuss *teachers as writers*. You may find out that some of your team already write, in which case they can share their knowledge. Discuss ways to increase the writing output of the teachers, as well as the students.
- Nominate a group from your school to present at a state or national conference on a particularly successful unit of work or idea. This may require writing a conference abstract or a follow-up article for a journal or magazine.

Chapter 11: Creating a Culture of Writing

Like *Practical Reading Strategies*, this book was always intended to go beyond instruction and towards building a strong culture in English and across the curriculum. Throughout the book we have prioritised activities that are easy to adapt and apply, and which any teacher can pick up and run with. When building a culture of writing across the school, however, it is necessary to take a bigger-picture view.

In *PRS*, Leon discussed creating a culture of reading through both a strategic approach to planning the curriculum and through some 'big events' to celebrate reading. This book takes a similar view of writing. It is necessary to develop a clear vision and strategy from improving writing across the whole school. There are also many events and activities that can be carried out outside of the classroom to add value to the writing process.

This chapter explores a few ways to build on the Writing Strategies and create a culture of writing that extends beyond the classroom.

Develop a shared vision

Why is writing important to you, your faculty and your school? Why is it important to your students? Developing a shared vision for writing involves pinning down the 'why'. In Chapter 6 we discussed the purpose of writing as we see it – a purpose that extends far beyond assessments and outcomes. You will need to work with your team to develop a shared vision for what writing means in your context. The process is the same as the one outlined in *PRS*.

Starting with a small group of teachers – perhaps a subgroup of the English faculty – develop a vision for writing in the school. Gather data on current writing habits, for surveying teachers on how much class time is spent writing, interviewing students and parents, or surveying cohorts of students to identify how frequently they write, and what they are writing. Once you have the information on current writing habits, ask yourselves *why do we want to improve our writing culture?* This could be for any number of reasons. Maybe writing results have taken a hit over the past few years, in line with national statistics. Maybe you see improving writing as a way to improve engagement and results across the curriculum. Whatever your purpose, it should be unique to your school and your cohort of students.

Ask yourselves:

- How, when and what do our students currently write?
- Why do we want to improve the writing culture at our school?
- What outcomes would we expect to see if we improved the writing culture?
- Who are the key stakeholders in improving the culture? The teachers? The students? The parents?
- What tactics and strategies will we use to improve the writing culture?
- What can we control? What is out of our control?
- How will we know that we have started to improve the writing culture?

Once you have answered some of these questions, consider how the vision for improving the writing culture sits in the 'bigger picture', for example, as part of the English faculty goals or the school's strategic intent. The more comfortably the writing culture sits within the bigger systems of the school, the more likely it will be to stick.

Once you have a vision, investigate possibilities for improving the culture, such as those that follow.

Creative writing competitions

Creative writing competitions come in many forms, from in-house to national and even international contests. If you subscribe to mailing lists from publishers, you will get frequent updates for competitions that might be suitable for your students. It is useful to have a staff member who will be responsible for supporting students who enter competitions. This could be a teacher, head of faculty, library staff or anyone at your school who has an interest in writing.

In-house writing competitions might take place across year levels or within a cohort. You could choose an annual theme, or borrow a theme from an event like National Book Week. If you are hosting an in-house competition, try to enlist the principal, parents or other members of the community to help with the judging.

Role modelling writing

Just as teachers should model reading, it is very beneficial for students to see teachers writing. We expanded on this in Chapter 10 when we discussed teachers as writers. When students see their teachers publishing writing – whether fiction or nonfiction – it can be very motivating. These teachers would also make excellent judges for the writing competitions discussed above, bringing extra credibility to the panel.

Writing workshops

Writing workshops, like book clubs, could be held in a library or shared space at lunchtimes or before and after school. They provide an opportunity for budding writers to share their work and show a school's commitment to the writing process. Writing workshops also provide great material for entering competitions.

There are many resources online to help you structure a writing workshop. They can be as formal or informal as you like and could be led by either the students or a member of staff. Some schools also have writing workshops exclusively for teachers to support those who would like to write professionally.

Author engagement

Authors are a great resource to help build a culture of writing. Writers of all kinds – from young adult authors to journalists – are often available to run presentations and workshops in schools. Workshops on creative writing are a fun and engaging way to help build culture at any year level. Senior students might benefit from visits where the author talks through the writing process of a text they are studying. In the junior year levels, more interactive workshops might have students writing their own poetry, flash fiction or short stories under the guidance of a published author.

Try to vary the authors you have visit your school to represent the diverse range of texts studied across year levels. Choose authors who will appeal to specific cohorts and address strategic needs. For example, if you know from your data that there is a literacy gap between boys and girls in the middle years, consider finding an author who might appeal to those boys.

School anthologies

In stage six of the Writing Cycle, *Publication*, we outlined different ways to publish student work. Of these, school anthologies probably do the most to celebrate your school's culture of writing. We've seen great examples of school writing anthologies used to fundraise and as seasonal gifts, for example, end-of-year or Christmas anthologies of writing. Some schools have developed a longstanding tradition of an annual publication. These anthologies allow students from all year levels to contribute and demonstrate their best writing across a variety of forms.

Practical strategies for this chapter

Here are a few things you can do right now in your faculty and school leadership teams to create a culture of writing:

- Follow the vision advice above and write out a school strategy for improving the culture of writing.
- Seek out local printers or meet with your school development or marketing team and discuss the practicalities of publishing a print anthology.
- Find out if you have any published authors in your alumni community.
- Seek out teachers' associations for opportunities for teachers to write and publish, and share those resources with the staff.

Chapter 12: The Future of Writing

We don't have a crystal ball, but there are certain trends in education right now that might have an impact on the future of writing. Two of these – an increased shift towards capabilities and skills over content, and the increasing ubiquity of artificial intelligence (AI) – are worthy of further discussion.

Viewing writing through a competency lens

Schools are increasingly shifting their attention away from traditional subject-based education towards the assessment and valuing of broader competencies. Depending on where you look, these might be called 21st-century skills, the 6 Cs, or the general capabilities. Whatever particular language your school uses to describe these skills, they generally include a combination of the following:

- Ethical understanding
- Creativity and innovation
- Critical thinking and problem-solving

- Collaboration and teamwork
- Social and emotional
- Character and resilience
- Agency and voice
- Personal growth and wellbeing

Writing can be a valid part of all these areas, meaning that teaching the skills of writing remains important in spite of shifting educational trends. Schools are faced with the difficult problem of knowing how to assess these intangible skills, and writing – as well as discussion, demonstration through practice and observation – forms an important part of the assessment narrative.

Learner profiles are becoming increasingly common, demonstrating not only the academic achievement of the student, but the whole picture. In many cases, learner profiles are being promoted as a way to upend our reliance on high-stakes testing. We think that this can only be a good thing, and that having students able to express these competencies through writing will allow them to demonstrate their capabilities in a range of areas.

We're not alone in thinking this. The Australian Curriculum general capabilities discuss the relevance of critical and creative thinking, ethical and intercultural understanding, and personal and social capabilities with regards to English (ACARA, 2022). In particular, there is a focus on the "development of communication skills needed for analysis, research and the expression of viewpoints and argument", and the idea that "creative thinking enables students to apply imaginative and inventive capacities in the creation of their own original works".

In terms of the Writing Cycle and the activities in this book, we have already pointed out the similarities between the Writing Cycle and the design thinking process, frequently used to promote critical and creative thinking. The application of the Writing Cycle can help students produce work that evidence many of these skills and capabilities, for example:

Ethical understanding

Students explore texts that present ethical dilemmas, such as case studies in Religious Education, Humanities or Health classes. Using the mentor texts, they study the structure of arguments, lines of logic and techniques used to express the attitudes and positions presented by various authors.

Collaboration and teamwork

The fifth stage of the cycle offers an excellent opportunity to observe and offer feedback on a student's capacity to work with others. See Chapter 8 for ideas on how to assess the collaboration stage.

Agency and voice

Writing offers a unique opportunity for students to express themselves and to develop and strengthen their own voice. Although spoken words have a power of their own, writing is a powerful tool for clarifying and articulating ideas. Being able to write in an appropriate structure, style and voice for a given audience is a valuable skill.

Personal growth and wellbeing

The positive impacts of writing are well documented. Still, even journaling and diary writing is not as simple as just 'picking up a pen and writing whatever is in your head'. Students need support in developing habits around writing, and in developing confidence in personal writing.

Writing is not always the most appropriate outcome, nor is it the most suitable assessment tool for every student. But there are many instances where the skills of writing are highly appropriate for demonstrating these hard-to-assess skills.

AI and machine writing

At the time of publication, AI writing apps are prevalent in the media, closely following on the heels of AI image-generation apps such as DALL-E and Stable Diffusion. Although these apps aren't perfect, they can do a decent job of reproducing humanlike writing in a variety of forms.

There are important ethical concerns over AI, including with the large language models (LLMs) that underpin the writing tech. These range from privacy concerns to copyright infringement, and even the use of low-paid labour and the environmental impact of the technologies. This book isn't the place for these discussions, but Kate Crawford's (2021) *Atlas of AI* is an excellent resource if you're interested in the ethics of AI.

There are two areas which we think will have an impact on the future of writing in schools.

'Spinners', paraphrasing and plagiarism

The current most prominent use of these programmes in education is, sadly, cheating. The rise of AI paraphrasing apps, sometimes called 'spinners', is concerning in both secondary and tertiary education. Spinners take any text and reformulate it into a paraphrased passage. We have seen these used by students in tertiary studies where students are required to provide summaries of their readings. We have also seen them used by students in the Humanities and Sciences subjects in secondary school. The paraphrased output is unique and therefore passes plagiarism tests, making them hard to spot.

As well as spinners, many free and pay-per-word sites offer complete essay-writing services, which are underpinned by LLMs – 'deep learning' models, which reproduce language using a large data set. Most of these operate on the same premise: the user inputs an essay title and the software assembles content from the data set into a unique text. Here's an example body paragraph, based on the following prompt:

Write a 700-word essay about the following topic: 'How does Jane Austen view the sanctity of marriage in *Pride and Prejudice*?' Academic tone. Use short, inline quotes from the novel as evidence and explain the quotes without saying 'in this quote'. Sophisticated responses, graduate or postgraduate level. Focus on the author's craft.

> One of the main themes in the novel is the social pressure for women to marry for financial security and social status. When Elizabeth visits Charlotte Lucas, her friend tells her, "Happiness in marriage is entirely a matter of chance" (Austen 33). This statement highlights the lack of romantic expectations for marriage, as Charlotte sees it simply as a means of achieving financial stability. Furthermore, when Elizabeth rejects Mr. Collins' proposal, he tries to persuade her by saying, "My reasons for marrying are, first, that I think it a right thing for every clergyman in easy circumstances...to set the example of matrimony in his parish" (Austen 39). Mr. Collins' motives for marriage are not based on love or personal happiness, but rather on societal expectations and duty.
> (Written using ChatGPT (OpenAI, 2022))

The AI makes frequent errors, which can be picked up by an assessor with a keen (or even not-so-keen) eye. Because of the way these AI writers work, they frequently trip themselves up, inventing characters, fabricating references and getting important details totally wrong. But like the spinners, these apps produce unique writing, which can pass a plagiarism test, meaning that detection – for now – remains the purview of the human assessor.

These technologies raise an interesting question, and one which we have already addressed elsewhere in this book: what is the point of writing? When students can hit a button to generate a passable essay, what is the value in teaching essay writing? Similarly, once the technology is sufficiently advanced to create compelling stories, does that make the teaching of creative writing redundant? Of course not. But it does mean that we must rethink how and why we teach writing.

We said at the start of the chapter that we don't have a crystal ball. There are, however, some futures that suggest themselves to us. From most pessimistic to most optimistic, here are a few:

- **Scenario 1:** Acknowledging that students can go online and get free AI-written essays, the education system responds by a total ban on technology – a little like banning phones in classrooms because they're distracting, rather than educating students on the appropriate use of technology. All essays must now be written by hand, preferably under timed conditions. The system rejects AI, like antibodies attacking a foreign object.
- **Scenario 2:** Schools adopt a blended approach where students must draft extensively by hand and in class before being allowed to type up final essays. Final submissions are checked against drafted materials closely and at great expense to teacher time to authenticate work. Some students are canny enough to know that a teacher with more than 20 students in a class can't be watching everything all the time and copying an AI essay by hand as a 'first draft' is very tempting.
- **Scenario 3:** Teachers acknowledge that the problem isn't going away any time soon. We start directing our teaching more towards the purpose(s) of essay writing, and the ethics of cheating. Knowing that for some students the essay will never be an appropriate form of assessment, we find alternate ways to check their knowledge and skills.
- **Scenario 4:** AI writing replaces human writing for most functional uses. Writing is still taught as an expressive art, as something with mental health benefits, and as a tool for articulating thought and communicating. It is no longer used just as a form of assessment.

In reality, we can imagine something between scenarios 3 and 4. The technology really isn't going away and will continue to develop and evolve, and at an increasingly rapid pace. Ultimately, we are optimistic that writing will continue to play a role in both the assessment of complex, intangible competencies and in sync with advances in technology.

In terms of using the technology itself, we suggest that teachers get in and experiment, but remain mindful of the broader ethical, political and social concerns that are inextricably woven into the technology. By way of experimentation, we used OpenAI's GPT-3 program to co-author some of the materials for examples and mentor texts. In our case, this involved using the technology to create unique texts from composites of student work (with permission from the students) and generating original text using prompts.

The aforementioned concerns about copyright gave us good cause to hesitate, but we are both agreed that the technology is not going away, and that it is down to us to get a handle on how and when it might be used in an educational setting.

Practical strategies for this chapter

You don't have a crystal ball, but there are a few ways you can work with your team towards the future of writing in education:

- Familiarise yourself with the ethical and practical concerns of AI, both in and outside of education.
- Sign up for a couple of free AI writing tools and explore the various approaches to essay writing, creative writing and procedural writing or list-making. Consider if, when and how you might incorporate some of these into your units of work.
- As a faculty or school, draft a policy on plagiarism and the use of AI-writing software. Discuss whether you will ban the technologies outright (difficult to control) or teach students responsible use and acknowledgement.
- Discuss where English and the instruction of writing sits in broader frameworks, such as the general capabilities or '21st-century skills'. Interview students and find their opinions (see Chapter 6 on the purpose of writing).

Conclusion

When Leon wrote *Practical Reading Strategies*, it was mainly as a way of capturing all the hard work that had gone into developing a reading curriculum. There was a team of English teachers driving the change at our school, and an even larger community as part of the VATE research project. *Practical Writing Strategies* was an altogether different process. We had no Community of Practice to lean on (although VATE has launched a Writing programme for 2023), and so we had to rely on our own research skills to navigate down the rabbit hole of writing instruction.

Writing is just as complex a process as reading in terms of the demands on students, and the demands on those teaching the skills. We found that there is no universally agreed upon best practice – it is something which, as 90% of the articles we read stated, "needs further research". Nonetheless, we identified as much of 'what works' as possible, and then proceeded to try it out with our students. Along the way, we learned a lot.

If you read *PRS*, then you'll already know Leon's opinions on formulaic and assessment-driven practices in schools. Ben, who is now taking on Leon's position at Monivae College as Director of Learning and Teaching, shares those opinions. Writing instruction should be freed from the demands of high-stakes examinations and brought back into the realm of creativity, expression and the kind of rewarding mental effort we should expect from our entire education system.

Throughout this book, we hope you have found some activities that you can use immediately in your classrooms. However, what we'd really like to see is you adapting and adjusting the activities to suit your needs. What surprised Leon the most about *PRS* was how the English teacher community picked up the activities and ran with them. From writing Design Thinking units based on the *PRS* Strategies to adapting visual tasks for Shakespeare to adopting the approaches as part of whole-school literacy programmes, teachers have taken the first book and given it a life of its own.

We hope that the same thing happens with *PWS*.

Leon Furze and Benjamin White

References

Applebee, AN (1984). 'Writing and Reasoning.' *Review of Educational Research, 54*(4), 577–596. https://doi.org/10.3102/00346543054004577

Australian Curriculum, Assessment and Reporting Authority (ACARA) (2022). *General Capabilities in the Australian Curriculum: English.* https://docs.acara.edu.au/resources/English_-_GC_learning_area.pdf

Australian Education Research Organisation (AERO) Ltd (2022). *Writing and writing instruction: An overview of the literature.* edresearch.edu.au

Australian Education Research Organisation (2022b). *Writing development: What does a decade of NAPLAN data reveal?* edresearch.edu.au

Bernot, A (2022). 'Not Big Brother, but close: a surveillance expert explains some of the ways we're all being watched, all the time.' The Conversation. www.theconversation.com/not-big-brother-but-close-a-surveillance-expert-explains-some-of-the-ways-were-all-being-watched-all-the-time-194917

Boscolo, P, & Gelati, C (2008). 'Motivating reluctant students to write: Suggestions and caveats.' *Insights on Learning Disabilities, 5*(2), 61–74

Carey, MD, Davidow, S, & Williams, P (2022). 'Re-imagining narrative writing and assessment: a post-NAPLAN craft-based rubric for creative writing.' *The Australian Journal of Language and Literacy*, 45(1), 33-48. https://doi.org/10.1007/s44020-022-00004-4

Chapman, ML (1999). 'Situated, social, active.' *Written Communication*, 16(4), 469–490. https://doi.org/10.1177/0741088399016004003

Crawford, K (2021). *Atlas of AI: Power, Politics, and the Planetary Costs of Artificial Intelligence*. Yale University Press

Derewianka, BM (2015). *The contribution of genre theory to literacy education in Australia*

Derewianka, B, & Jones, P (2016). *Teaching Language in Context*. Oxford University Press

Gee, JP (2004). *Situated language and learning*. https://doi.org/10.4324/9780203594216

Gillespie, A, Graham, S, Kiuhara, S, & Hebert, M (2013). 'High school teachers use of writing to support students' learning: a national survey.' *Reading and Writing*, 27(6), 1043–1072. https://doi.org/10.1007/s11145-013-9494-8

Graham, S, & Hebert, M (2010). *Writing to Read: Evidence for How Writing can Improve Reading*. A report from Carnegie Corporation of New York

Graham, S, McKeown, D, Kiuhara, S, & Harris, KR (2012). 'A meta-analysis of writing instruction for students in the elementary grades.' *Journal of Educational Psychology*, 104(4), 879–896. https://doi.org/10.1037/a0029185

Graham, S (2018). 'A Revised Writer(s)-Within-Community Model of Writing.' *Educational Psychologist*, 53(4), 258–279. https://doi.org/10.1080/00461520.2018.1481406

Graham, S (2020). 'The Sciences of Reading and Writing Must Become More Fully Integrated.' *Reading Research Quarterly*, 55(S1). https://doi.org/10.1002/rrq.332

Hebert, M, Simpson, A, & Graham, S (2012). 'Comparing effects of different writing activities on reading comprehension: A meta-analysis.' *Reading and Writing*, 26(1), 111–138. https://doi.org/10.1007/s11145-012-9336-3

Hermansson, C, & Lindgren, E (2019). 'Writing as a cognitive process.' Cambridge English. World of Better Learning | Cambridge University Press. www.cambridge.org/elt/blog/2019/12/19/writing-cognitive-process/#:~:text=Writing%20is%20a%20very%20complex,while%20simultaneously%20writing%20a%20text

McKnight, L (2020). 'Since feeling is first: the art of teaching to write paragraphs.' *English in Education, 55*(1), 37-52. https://doi.org/10.1080/04250494.2020.1768069

McKnight, L (2020b). 'Teaching writing by formula: empowerment or exclusion?' *International Journal of Inclusive Education*, 1-15. https://doi.org/10.1080/13603116.2020.1864790

Moon, B (2011). *Writing Projects 2: Practical lessons based on classical methods.* Chalkface Press

Newell, GE (2006). 'Writing to Learn: How Alternative Theories of School Writing Account for Student Performance.' *Handbook of writing research*, 235-247

OpenAI (2022). *ChatGPT.* https://chat.openai.com/chat

Richards, JC, & Reppen, R (2014). 'Towards a Pedagogy of Grammar Instruction.' *RELC Journal, 45*(1), 5-25. https://doi.org/10.1177/0033688214522622

Ritchhart, R, & Church, M (2020). *The Power of Making Thinking Visible: Practices to Engage and Empower all Learners.* John Wiley & Sons

Serravallo, J (2015). *The Reading Strategies Book: Your Everything Guide to Developing Skilled Readers.* Heinemann Educational Books

Shanahan, T, & Shanahan, C (2012). 'What is disciplinary literacy and why does it matter?' *Topics in Language Disorders, 32*(1), 7-18. https://doi.org/10.1097/tld.0b013e318244557a

Tamang, S (2020). 'Opinion: Without communities, conservation fails in eastern Himalayas (Red pandas and pangolins).' The Third Pole. www.thethirdpole.net/en/regional-cooperation/red-panda-pangolin-conservation-eastern-himalayas

Tovani, C (2004). *Do I Really Have to Teach Reading?: Content Comprehension, Grades 6-12.* Stenhouse Publishers

Tovani, C (2011). *So What Do They Really Know?: Assessment That Informs Teaching and Learning.* Stenhouse Publishers

www.ingramcontent.com/pod-product-compliance
Lightning Source LLC
Chambersburg PA
CBHW050417120526
44590CB00015B/2005